CLASSICAL COMICS

TEACHING RESOURCE PACK

Making the classics accessible
for teachers and students

Suitable for teaching ages 10-17

Written by: Neil Bowen

Frankenstein

THE GRAPHIC NOVEL

Mary Shelley

CLASSICAL COMICS TEACHING RESOURCE PACK

Frankenstein

Perfect bound edition published 2018
First published 2009

Published by: Classical Comics Ltd

Written by: Neil Bowen
Character Designs & Original Artwork: Declan Shalvey
Art Director: Jon Haward
Coloring: Jason Cardy & Kat Nicholson
Design & Layout: Jo Wheeler & Jenny Placentino
Editor in Chief: Clive Bryant

Acknowledgments: Every effort has been made to trace copyright holders of material reproduced in this book. Any rights not acknowledged here will be acknowledged in subsequent editions if notice is given to Classical Comics Ltd.

All enquiries should be addressed to:
Classical Comics Ltd.
PO Box 7280
LUDLOW
SY8 9DL
United Kingdom
Tel: +44 (0)845 812 3000

education@classicalcomics.com
www.classicalcomics.com

ISBN: 978-1-907127-77-9

Printed in the USA

CONTENTS

INTRODUCTION

WELCOME TO THE *FRANKENSTEIN* TEACHING RESOURCE FROM CLASSICAL COMICS.

As always with our teaching resources we aim to provide enough information to satisfy teachers and students alike, in the form of enjoyable activities that children will engage with and to make lessons engrossing as well as informing.

Because the exercises feature illustrations from the graphic novel, they provide an immediate link for students between the book and the exercise – however they can also be used in conjunction with any traditional text; and many of the activities can be used completely stand-alone.

Aimed at ages 10 and above, each book provides exercises that cover structure, listening, understanding, motivation and comprehension as well as key words, themes and literary techniques. Although the majority of the tasks focus on the use of language, you will also find many cross-curriculum topics, covering areas within history, IT, drama, reading, speaking, writing and art; and with a range of skill levels, they provide many opportunities for differentiated teaching and the tailoring of lessons to meet individual needs.

These widely acclaimed books are designed by teachers, for teachers, to help you meet curriculum guidelines.

If you have any feedback, comments or suggestions that will enhance this book, please email them to education@classicalcomics.com.

Your thoughts and input are always appreciated.
Classical Comics Ltd

"It was the secrets of heaven and earth I desired to learn" Victor Frankenstein

Neil Bowen has taught in a wide variety of schools and is currently Head of English at Wells Cathedral School, in Somerset, England. He is the author of many articles on Literature and English resources. He writes, he says, "lamentable" poetry in his spare time and he continues to work on his great unpublished post modern novel; a sort of *Ulysses* meets *Bravo Two Zero* via *Frankenstein* Gothic Magic Realist action adventure story. He is also an "A" level examiner for OCR, the South West England co-ordinator for NATE, and a keen cricketer.

MARY SHELLEY
1797-1851

"It is not singular that, as the daughter of two persons of distinguished literary celebrity, I should very early in life have thought of writing."

Mary Shelley was born in London in 1797, into an exceptionally gifted, intellectual family. Her mother, Mary Wollstonecraft, was a famous radical writer, and her father was the philosopher William Godwin. Mary Wollstonecraft's *Vindication of the Rights of Women* is an important early feminist work. In this she argued that women should no longer be treated as second-class citizens. Just as influential was her father, Godwin, whose liberal philosophy was fundamental in shaping the political views of a generation of writers and thinkers.

Given this family, it is not very surprising that Mary Shelley was supremely talented, or that she would follow the life of a writer. From an early age, however, love and death were intimately linked in Mary's life; tragically Mary Wollstonecraft died giving birth to her daughter.

By any standards Mary Shelley's early adulthood was a life lived in the extreme.

At just **17** she eloped to the continent with lover Percy Bysshe Shelley, the radical romantic poet.

When Mary was **18** she gave birth prematurely to a daughter. Sadly the baby died only a few days later.

By the time she was **19** Mary had given birth to a son, William, and written her first and most famous novel *Frankenstein*.

BIRTH OF A NOVEL

In the rainy summer of 1816 Mary was visiting Geneva with Shelley. In particular they visited Villa Diodati, where the infamous Romantic poet Lord Byron was living. Like Shelley, Byron was a free-spirited, fiery poet exiled from England. Leaving behind him a celebrated public scandal, Byron had been labelled by his ex-lover, Lady Caroline Lamb as "mad, bad and dangerous to know". A sense of his extraordinary character is also clear from his unusual housemate during his time at Cambridge. In his rooms Byron apparently kept a tame bear.

One evening at the villa, after a prolonged rainy period spent reading German ghost stories, Byron suddenly announced that "we will each write a ghost story". At first Mary could think of nothing to write. In contrast, Shelley was straight to work, and Byron began a piece that later would be worked up by his physician, John Polidori, into one of the first vampire stories in English, *The Vampyre: A Tale.*

Days passed and still Mary had nothing.

Conversation in Byron's home must have been exciting though; some of the most radical ideas of the age were batted about between Byron and Shelley. One idea, in particular, had stuck in Mary's imagination and now slowly began to grow.

In her own introduction to *Frankenstein* Mary refers to discussing whether "the component parts of a creature might be manufactured, brought together and endued* with vital warmth". And when she went to bed one evening, unable to sleep, in her tortured half-waking, half-sleeping state a vision came to her out of the night:

"I saw the pale student of unhallowed arts kneeling beside the thing he had put together. I saw the hideous phantasm of a man stretched out, and then, on the working of some powerful engine, show signs of life, and stir with an uneasy, half-vital motion".

From this half-dream, half-nightmare sprung the idea for a novel that would become famous the world over, *Frankenstein.*

Ten months later and Mary was married to Shelley, living back in England, celebrating the completion of her novel.

Aged just **21** Mary had *Frankenstein* published, had given birth to another baby daughter and seen this daughter die.

By the time she was **22** more tragedy had struck with the death of her beloved son, William.

In 1822, when she was **25**, the series of tragedies was complete. Her husband, Shelley, set sail in a terrible storm and died at sea.

In 1824 she wrote in her journal:
"At the age of twenty six I am in the condition of an aged person--all my old friends are gone ... & my heart fails when I think by how few ties I hold to the world...."

The rest of her life may have been less tempestuous and dramatic, but Mary continued to write and to look after her one surviving child, Percy. She died in London in 1851 and is buried with her mother and father in St.Peter's churchyard, Bournemouth.

*** The word Mary Shelley was looking for is "imbue", which means to permeate, or inspire. That she got the spelling so wrong shows that even great writers can't always spell very well!**

FRANKENSTEIN AND THE GOTHIC NOVEL

Mary Shelley's novel is part of a group of work that can be defined as "gothic". The first of these books was Horace Walpole's novel *The Castle of Otranto*, published in 1764. The success of this supernatural tale led to a number of other similar *Tales of Terror* being published, culminating in *Frankenstein* in 1818.

After this gothic novels declined in popularity with both writers and readers. Until, that is, the Victorian period when there was a second flowering. Between 1880 and the end of the century a host of important novels were published and widely read. These include R.L. Stevenson's sinister *The Strange Case of Doctor Jekyll and Mister Hyde*, and Bram Stoker's thrilling epic, *Dracula*.

The first wave of gothic novels had a number of distinct characteristics:

- They include the supernatural, ghosts and spirits as well as spooky creepy settings, such as old castles or churches.
- They attempt to induce feelings of horror, fear or terror in the reader.
- They show an interest in the return of something buried from the past.
- They feature monstrous villains often chasing beautiful, virtuous heroines.

In some ways Shelley deviates from these gothic conventions. For example, instead of an ancient castle, Victor isolates himself in his laboratory; and where other early gothic books would feature a ghostly figure, Shelley has a towering monster. She was also original in her characterization. Victor Frankenstein, the mad scientist, who will do anything to make a breakthrough discovery, is quite different from the villains or heroes in the other books. And in this character Shelley started a long line of mad scientists in fiction, from Dr Jekyll through to Bruce Bannister.

Indeed in her exploration of the possibilities of science and its potential dangers, as well as in her creation of the first "alien" creature, Shelley also developed a new sort of literature, today known as "science fiction".

A quick look in your local bookshop or library will confirm that the gothic is once again a popular genre, particularly in children's and young adult fiction. As well as *Goosebumps* and *A Series of Unfortunate Events* for younger readers, there are the best selling "Darren Shan" books and their many imitators.

QUESTIONS:

Write your answers on a separate sheet of paper.

1. What is it, do you think, that continues to make gothic novels popular?

2. Do they offer anything more than the cheap thrills of a fairground ghost train?

3. How are gothic novels different from horror novels?

TASK:

In groups of four sketch out and plan a gothic novel, or film. You will need to create a main character, and some form of supernatural opponent, or villain. You will also need a spooky setting, perhaps a chase scene, and a climax where good and evil face each other and fight.

SCIENCE FICTION OR SCIENCE FACT?

One of the key ideas at work in Mary Shelley's novel is the creation of life from dead material. More specifically the idea is the reanimation of a corpse through the application of an electrical charge. Whilst this might seem evidence of Shelley's wild imagination, similar experiments had actually been undertaken during her lifetime.

An Italian scientist, Galvani, for instance, had applied electrical hooks to the corpse of a criminal who had been executed by hanging. After the first experiment Galvani reported excitedly that "the corpse's jaw began to quiver, and adjoining muscles were horribly contorted, and the left eye actually opened". In the end Galvani's research proved fruitless, but it is evidence of the world of discovery Shelley lived within and of humankind's continuing fascination with the idea of defeating death.

Another famous scientist of the age was Humphry Davy. A pioneer of electrochemistry, Davy discovered potassium and sodium. He was a friend of the poet Samuel Taylor Coleridge and the inventor of laughing gas. Apparently the two of them had some interesting evenings working on the gas! Humphry Davy was famously idealistic about science, writing that it had "done much for man, but was capable of doing still more". Some critics think the character of Frankenstein was based on Davy.

TASK:

Research the new discoveries being made by scientists in the early nineteenth century. Present your findings either orally, in a PowerPoint presentation or in the form of a poster.

WHO OR WHAT IS THE MONSTER?

Since its publication in 1818 Mary Shelley's novel has been interpreted in a range of different ways. Some readers, for instance, have used Shelley's own life to explore the novel. In particular the death of her mother, Mary Wollstonecraft, after giving birth to Mary, and the subsequent death of three of her own children has led these readers to see the novel as being about fears of childbirth and parenthood.

Read in this way there can be little doubt that Victor Frankenstein is a terrible father, abandoning his child because it is hideous and leaving it to lead a life of suffering. The creature's bitterness is then understandable.

SCIENCE FICTION OR SCIENCE FACT?

Another interesting interpretation connects the novel to when and where it was written. Crucial to your understanding of this period is a little information about one of the most bloody and significant events in European history.

THE FRENCH REVOLUTION

In 1789 a people's revolution broke out in France sweeping before it the old order of the aristocratic ruling classes and their King, Louis XVI. You may have heard of his sensitive wife, Marie Antoinette, who when told that the starving masses had no bread to eat, famously said, "well let them eat cake!". By 1792 the King was in jail and a new Republican government in place. Their slogan, "Liberty, Equality, Fraternity" seemed to ring out across Europe, a symbol of a new more hopeful, fairer world.

Initially, in England, radical writers and thinkers, such as Mary's father, William Godwin celebrated the overthrow of oppression and the freeing of the French people. The romantic poet, William Wordsworth wrote, "Bliss was it then to be alive. To be young was a very heaven". Attitudes changed, however, when the glorious revolution turned to nightmare.

THE GUILLOTINE AND THE TERROR

During the September Massacres of 1792 approximately 1400 men and women were slaughtered by revolutionaries in Paris alone, with similar massacres taking place in many other French cities. In 1793 Louis XVI was executed, beheaded by the infamous guillotine.

That year Maximilien Robespierre became France's leader and things just kept getting worse. What followed was an extraordinary period of violent bloodshed, with anyone who disagreed with the new government carted off to the guillotine to be beheaded. This period is known simply as "The Terror".

HOW DOES THIS RELATE TO *FRANKENSTEIN*?

The contemporary politician, Edmund Burke, memorably said that "out of the tomb of the murdered monarchy in France has arisen a vast, tremendous, deformed spectre".

Shelley's novel can thus be read as a "Gothicized" story of the French Revolution. For example Victor Frankenstein's idealism, his desire to create a new, better race of men could represent the idealism of the French Revolutionaries who wanted to make a better, fairer society.

TASK 1:
Looking at Mary Shelley's life, what do you think the monster might represent?

TASK 2:
What happened in the year 1816 that may have influenced the story?

SOMETHING WICKED THIS WAY COMES

MONSTERS

Staz Johnson

Frankenstein's creature is only one of the many monsters that feature in literature and film. In literature there is a very long line of monsters stretching back over hundreds, even thousands of years. The Greek myths are a particularly rich source. Wandering through these ancient stories are cyclops, hydras, Medusa, the Minotaur, harpies, the chimera and a host of others too gruesome to mention. Folk and fairy tales also often feature monsters, such as the witch, the giant and the wolf.

Other famous monsters include vampires, especially Dracula, Grendel, Mr. Hyde, werewolves, mummies, zombies, King Kong, Alien, the Abominable Snowman, Orcs and Godzilla. Fantasy superhero comics, such as those published by Marvel and DC are also full of monsters, from The Green Goblin to Mephisto. Science Fiction has spawned a few memorable examples. Just think of Dr. Who and his adversaries – the Daleks or the Cybermen. Everywhere you look in films and books there seem to be monsters lumbering around generally being unpleasant and threatening!

Staz Johnson

What is it, do you think, that makes monsters such a popular feature of stories?
One of the main functions of monsters is to provide contrast to humans. By knowing what is monstrous we are more able to define what is human. In the case of zombies, for example, these creatures may, superficially look human(ish), but their complete inability to think and make rational or moral decisions highlights these abilities in human characters.

Arguably the most frightening monsters are those that most closely resemble human beings. Mr. Hyde in Robert Louis Stevenson's Victorian novella is violent and brutal, and although there is something horrible about his appearance, he is somehow also anonymous and can vanish into a crowd, a trick much harder for an Orc or a werewolf. Hyde can therefore walk amongst us, his villainy hidden, but ready to break out into murderous violence at any moment. Linked to this idea of the closeness between monsters and humans is the idea of transformation, or metamorphosis. Metamorphosis of good characters into their evil side is a regular feature in characterization of monsters. Just as the upright Dr. Jekyll transforms into the murderous Mr. Hyde, so timid Bruce Bannister when very angry turns into the Incredible Hulk, or if there's a full moon nice Professor Lupin turns into a voracious werewolf, Spider-man becomes Venom and so on.

Transformation suggests that in certain conditions we may lose control of ourselves and unleash "the beast within". Neatly it also returns us to where we began this section. One of the most famous and influential collections of Ancient Greek stories of monsters and men, was Ovid's *Metamorphosis,* a collection well worth dipping into. You may find a modern version more accessible than the Latin! Ted Hughes' *Tales from Ovid* are particularly dramatic and exciting…

TASK:

Imagine you have been asked to devise a really frightening monster for a gothic film about genetic engineering gone wrong. Working with a partner, come up with ideas for your monster. Include some pictures, written descriptions and ideas for how to present them in the film.

CHAPTER-BY-CHAPTER

VOLUME ONE

Letter I
"Some great purpose"
We meet the polar adventurer, Walton. We learn of his hungry curiosity and limitless ambition. In his letter to his sister, Margaret, Walton explains how he has been enchanted by the mysterious and unmapped North Pole, and how, by going there, he plans to make a breakthrough discovery about magnetism: "I may there discover the wondrous power which attracts the needle".

Letter II
"The want of a friend"
Walton tells his sister about the crew of his ship and his own education. He reveals how he has been attracted to adventure and discovery by his "love of the marvellous". This is why he is drawn to "the wild sea and unvisited regions".

Letter III
"What can stop the determined heart and resolved will of man?"
Walton feels confident. All is going well as his ship sails toward the North Pole and adventure.

Letter IV
"Brother of my heart"

1. Having reached the outer regions of the pole, Walton is astonished to see the "gigantic" "shape of a man" whizzing across the ice in a sledge. Soon after, the exhausted figure of Victor Frankenstein is hauled aboard. He is barely alive, having been tracking the "demon". Walton nurses Frankenstein back to health and recognizes his unusual nobility of spirit.

2. Walton tells his new companion that "I would sacrifice my fortune, my existence, my every hope, to the furtherance of my enterprise". Frankenstein listens in increasing gloom. Frankenstein tells Walton of a friend who has died.

3. Frankenstein says that he will tell Walton his whole story, and that he should be warned by it.

CHAPTER-BY-CHAPTER FRANKENSTEIN'S STORY

Chapter 1
"My more than sister"
Frankenstein begins his story with his father and mother. He tells Walton he was born into a wealthy, aristocratic family, but that his father married Catherine, the poor daughter of a bankrupt friend. Frankenstein was the only child of the household until his mother rescued a beautiful orphan, Elizabeth, from a life of poverty.

Chapter 2
"It was the secrets of heaven and earth I desired to learn"
Frankenstein explains his privileged and happy childhood. As a child he becomes friends with an imaginative boy called Henry Clerval and also enjoys the company of Elizabeth, who he calls a "saintly soul". Slowly though, as he grows up, Victor becomes entranced by the idea of magic. In particular he dreams of "discovering life's greatest mysteries". He begins a feverish search for the philosopher's stone and for the "elixir of life".

Chapter 3
"A student at Ingolstadt"
Frankenstein's mother dies; her dying hope that Elizabeth and Frankenstein will marry. Victor leaves Geneva to become a student at Ingolstadt University. Like any new student, his first impressions of his teachers are mixed: "M.Kempe was a little squat man, with a gruff voice and a repulsive countenance". The Chemistry teacher, M.Waldman, is more impressive. Unlike some students, Frankenstein works like a devil.

Chapter 4
"The cause of generation and life"
Through endless solitary toil and labor, Frankenstein makes the remarkable discovery of the key to life, and his story accelerates. He begins to gather gruesome materials from graveyards and slaughterhouses. Isolated, alone, and near mad, he works maniacally day and night in his "workshop of filthy creation". His emotions veer from exultation at the wonderful thing he will create, to anxiety about his neglect of friends, family and his own health.

CHAPTER-BY-CHAPTER FRANKENSTEIN'S STORY

Chapter 5
"I saw the dull yellow eye of the creature open"
The creature he has constructed from corpses awakes. As from a sudden blow, Frankenstein recoils from the physical horror of his creation. He flees from his laboratory in fear and horror, only for the "wretch", the "demoniacal corpse" to follow him. Abandoning the creature, Frankenstein spends the night wandering the dismal streets of Ingolstadt, where, by pure chance he meets his old friend Henry Clerval. Henry is newly arrived from Geneva, ready to become a student at the University. The mixture of excitement and dread, coupled with physical exhaustion bring on a "nervous fever" and Frankenstein collapses. During several hard months Henry nurses his friend.

Chapter 6
"Dear, dear Elizabeth"
Frankenstein reads a letter sent to him from Elizabeth. She is anxious about his health and tells him about Justine, a young girl who has become part of the Frankenstein household, and of William his angelic little brother.

Back at Ingolstadt, Frankenstein introduces Clerval to his teachers and with him begins a study of Oriental languages. Time passes and Victor recovers his health to the extent that his "spirits were high" and he "bounded along with feelings of unbridled joy." He seems to have forgotten all about his creation.

Chapter 7
"William is dead!"
A letter from his father informs Victor of some terrible news; his little brother, William has been murdered. Frankenstein rushes home to Geneva. Any happiness he feels on returning to his "beloved country" is clouded by a sense of foreboding. During a violent storm in the Alps he spies the lumbering, gigantic figure of "the filthy daemon to whom I have given life." Anguished, Frankenstein realizes fully for the first time the true horror he has unleashed on humankind.

Arriving at his father's house Victor discovers that the young girl, Justine, is accused of William's murder.

Chapter 8
"The trial began"
Though innocent, and despite Elizabeth's powerful defense, Justine is tried and convicted for the murder of William. Frankenstein agonizes over his responsibility, but fears if he tells anyone they will think him mad. Justine is executed. The chapter, and Volume One, closes with Victor gazing at the graves of "William and Justine, the first hapless victims of my unhallowed arts".

CHAPTER-BY-CHAPTER FRANKENSTEIN'S STORY

VOLUME TWO

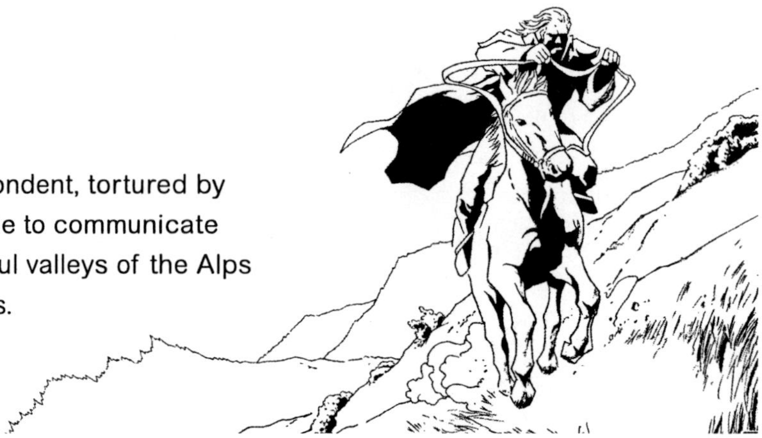

Chapter 1
"A scene of singular beauty"
Two months pass and Frankenstein is despondent, tortured by guilt. He feels isolated from his family, unable to communicate with them. He travels into one of the beautiful valleys of the Alps and begins to feel its gentle, curative effects.

Chapter 2
"You, my creator"
The following day the weather becomes stormy and Frankenstein's mood also darkens. Nevertheless he continues his solitary travels until he sees a huge being moving towards him with "superhuman speed". Frankenstein and the monster talk, and Victor is persuaded to visit the monster's hut to hear his story.

CHAPTER-BY-CHAPTER THE MONSTER'S STORY

Chapter 3
"The village was roused"
Frankenstein's creation tells of how he survived, first by foraging in a forest and then later by living in a hovel, adjoining a cottage. In between times he was beaten and chased away by frightened villagers. Through a chink in the wall between the hovel and the cottage he watched a family and slowly learnt from them.

Chapter 4
"The gentle manners and beauty of the cottagers"
The family he watches are poor and sometimes unhappy. The monster feels sorry for them, and when he can't be seen, during the night he begins to do little jobs such as gathering wood for them. He listens carefully to their words and learns some basic vocabulary.

Chapter 5
"What was I?"
The monster continues to learn from watching his gentle neighbors, picking up from them ideas about society, history and religion. These new ideas make him reflect miserably on his own status, the unloved lowest of the low.

CHAPTER-BY-CHAPTER
THE MONSTER'S STORY

Chapter 6

"I felt the greatest ardor for virtue rise within me"

Frankenstein is told about Felix, the young man of the family, his sister Agatha and their blind father. With Victor we hear of Felix's valor in saving a Turkish man from unjust imprisonment and of the Turk's betrayal of Felix. And we hear about the Turk's beautiful, noble daughter, Safie.

Chapter 7

"Great God," exclaimed the old man, "Who are you?"

Fortuitously the monster chances upon some books and reads them eagerly, so continuing his education. Again he reflects bitterly on being abandoned by his creator and yearns for companionship. Although he knows it will be difficult, he resolves to make himself known to the cottagers, trusting in their goodness to recognize beneath his horrible exterior the goodness of his heart. Finally when he does this Felix drives him away with a stick.

Chapter 8

"Cursed, cursed creator!"

Filled with rage and despair the monster sets off to revenge himself on Frankenstein. But the beautiful natural alpine landscape slowly eases his rage, so much so that when he sees a small girl fall into a fast-flowing stream and rescues her from drowning. His reward for this is to be shot at and wounded by the girl's father. Doubly enraged when later he stumbles upon young William Frankenstein he kills him. Then cunningly he plants some evidence on a sleeping girl (Justine) so that she will be blamed for the murder.

Chapter 8 ends with the monster making a demand to the appalled Frankenstein: Either he must make him a companion "as deformed and horrible as myself" or else suffer more death and misery.

Chapter 9

"If I have no ties and no affection, hatred and vice must be my portion"

The creature's arguments for justice, coupled with his promise to exile himself and his mate forever, far from humankind, overcome Frankenstein's revulsion at the thought of creating another monster. He promises to begin constructing a female monster, as soon as he can.

CHAPTER-BY-CHAPTER FRANKENSTEIN'S STORY

VOLUME THREE

Chapter 1
"The very poetry of nature"
Frankenstein leaves Elizabeth and his family to visit England and build his new female monster. Accompanying him on his travels is his excellent friend, Henry Clerval. If all goes well, Victor plans to marry Elizabeth.

Chapter 2
"I am a blasted tree"
He journeys through England and on to Scotland before arriving at a remote Orkney island. There, alone, he begins his gruesome work, haunted all the time by "obscure forebodings of evil".

Chapter 3
"(I) tore to pieces the thing on which I was engaged"
When the monster visits him to check on the progress of its mate, Frankenstein is appalled by the idea of releasing more evil into the world. Determinedly he destroys the creature he has been making. Watching him, the monster vows bitter revenge, warning "I shall be with you on your wedding night". Wearily Victor makes his journey back to England. Caught in stormy weather his boat is grounded in Ireland, where Frankenstein is promptly arrested for murder.

Chapter 4
"I lay for two months on the point of death"
In Ireland Frankenstein is charged with the murder of Henry Clerval, who has been found strangled. Shocked by his friend's death, Victor falls again into a fever. His father arrives to clear his name and rescue him. Cleared of the murder, Frankenstein sets sail homeward with his father.

Chapter 5
"One smile on your lips"
On his way home Frankenstein receives a letter from Elizabeth. She tells Victor how deeply she loves him and admits her fears that he is in love with someone else. In a letter to her he confides that he has a terrible secret, which he will tell her after they are married. Frankenstein is convinced he will be the victim of the monster's revenge, and, as his wedding night approaches he feels a familiar sense of dread.

Chapter 6
"I heard a shrill and dreadful scream"
On the night of their wedding Frankenstein paces about, expecting at any moment for the monster to attack him. Hearing a scream from the bedroom, where he has left Elizabeth, he rushes in to find his wife strangled, her body flung across the bed. Fearing more murders, he rushes back to Geneva. On hearing the news of Elizabeth's murder, Victor's father dies of heartache. Frankenstein determines to hunt down and destroy the monster.

CHAPTER-BY-CHAPTER FRANKENSTEIN'S STORY

Chapter 7
"Let him feel the despair"
At the graves of William and Elizabeth, Frankenstein hears the monster mocking him. He pursues the creature, but it evades him. For many months doggedly he follows its trail, across continents always northwards to the Arctic. In the lands of mist and snow he is discovered, half-dead by Walton, and we are back where the novel began.

Walton takes up the story again in letters addressed once more to his sister. The ship is in terrible peril. "Surrounded by mountains of ice", it is trapped and will be crushed to pieces. Its crew demand they return at the first opportunity to England. Frankenstein, who is dying, asks Walton to complete his mission and kill the monster.

After the death of Frankenstein, around midnight Walton is disturbed by noises from the cabin in which Victor's body lies. Entering he finds the monster kneeling over the body of its creator. The monster tells Walton of its wretchedness and suffering. Informing Walton that it plans to kill itself in the remotest wastes by throwing itself onto a funeral pyre, the monster leaps out of the cabin window and is soon "borne away, and lost in darkness and distance". And thus the novel ends.

TASK 1:

As you can see, we have chosen quotations from each chapter to summarize the action. Skim back through the book and see if you can find alternative, perhaps better, quotations.

TASK 2:

Try writing a summary of the whole story, but in only 60 words, or fewer if you can. Only include the really important information. Compare your version with others in your class. Did anyone manage the task?

TASK 3:

Now reduce your 60 words to as few as possible by

1. Cutting out function words, such as prepositions (on, at, over etc.) and articles (the, a, these).
2. Converting your piece into text script.

TASK 4:

Text your version of the novel to a friend who hasn't read it. You will have been successful if they are then able to give you the gist of Shelley's novel from your text!

VICTOR FRANKENSTEIN

Victor Frankenstein is the main character of the novel. Another more technical word for the main character is the protagonist. Typically in early gothic novels the protagonist is female, passive and entirely innocent. This sort of flat characterization tends to produce stereotypical characters. Victor's beloved, Elizabeth, fits this type pretty well, as she is entirely virtuous and also the victim of the monster. But, of course, she is only a secondary character in Mary Shelley's novel. Frankenstein is a more interesting, well-rounded and believable character. A clear indication of this is that whilst he has good characteristics, such as his incredible focus on his work, he also has flaws.

In fact the novel's subtitle, *The Modern Prometheus* subtly indicates this mixture of good and bad qualities in Victor. As a liberator of humankind Prometheus is a heroic character. But he is also a Titan who sinfully aspires to being God, and so he can be seen less favorably. (For more on the Prometheus myth, see page 62).

Frankenstein as a character also embodies the gothic theme of the return of something from the past. Although he comes from a wealthy, stable family, who have been associated with law and good order for generations, and despite living in a sensible, rational society, Frankenstein becomes obsessed with ancient magic. In particular he is drawn to the works of magicians and alchemists, such as Cornelius Agrippa, Paracelsus and Albertus Magnus, figures associated with the occult. Though he may appear to be using science, in Frankenstein's laboratory he is working at an ancient, perhaps, demonic form of magic; bringing the dead back to life.

QUESTIONS:

Write your answers on a separate sheet of paper.

1. What does Frankenstein wish to discover when studying at Inglostadt?

2. What do you think are Frankenstein's motives? List the ones you can think of.

3. Are Frankenstein's motives all good, or all bad, or are his motives mixed?

VICTOR FRANKENSTEIN

TASK 1:

From the list of adjectives pick the ones that you think best describe Victor Frankenstein. Once you have done this, see if you can find an example from the novel of Victor showing each quality. The first one has been completed for you. You may wish to add your own adjectives to the end of the list.

Adjective	Evidence
Intelligent	While still a student, Frankenstein makes a brilliant discovery about "the secret of life".
Proud	
Strong-willed	
Cruel	
Loving	
Gentle	
Easy-going	
Independent	
Immature	
Considerate	
Confident	
Vain	
Kind	
Timid	
Greedy	
Heroic	
Brave	
Ambitious	
Weak	
Friendly	

VICTOR FRANKENSTEIN

QUESTIONS:

Write your answers on a separate sheet of paper.

1. How well do you think Frankenstein treats Elizabeth and his family?

2. Frankenstein is often called an "over-reacher" by critics. This means he pushes things too far, and oversteps boundaries. At what point in the novel do you think Frankenstein oversteps the boundary between right and wrong?

3. In some ways the monster and Frankenstein are similar characters. Both are isolated from their fellow men, both are very intelligent and both become driven by revenge.

4. Why do you think Mary Shelley may have wanted her protagonist and his adversary to have similarities?

VICTOR FRANKENSTEIN

FURTHER EXPLORATIONS

EXTENSION TASK 1:

Some critics have suggested that the figure of Victor Frankenstein was based on Mary Shelley's husband, the Romantic poet Percy Bysshe Shelley. Like Frankenstein, Percy Shelley was a rebel, a radical and an idealist. He had, for example, been expelled from Oxford University for circulating a pamphlet on the *Necessity of Atheism*. In the novel, critics suggest, Mary was able to express criticism of her husband's romantic idealism and articulate her own more moderate views.

Research the life of Percy Shelley. See if you think he is like Victor. Then discuss what idealistic ideas the novel may be rejecting and whether it presents alternative ideas. This is a very demanding task, but also potentially very interesting.

A good place to start with research on Shelley is to read his great poem *Ode to the West Wind*, in which the wind symbolizes idealism. Here are the first stanzas:

I.

WILD West Wind, thou breath of Autumn's being,
Thou, from whose unseen presence the leaves dead
Are driven, like ghosts from an enchanter fleeing,

Yellow, and black, and pale, and hectic red,
Pestilence-stricken multitudes: O thou,
Who chariotest to their dark wintry bed

The wingèd seeds, where they lie cold and low,
Each like a corpse within its grave, until
Thine azure sister of the spring shall blow

Her clarion o'er the dreaming earth, and fill
(Driving sweet buds like flocks to feed in air)
With living hues and odors plain and hill:

Wild Spirit, which art moving everywhere;
Destroyer and preserver; hear, oh, hear!

(For those interested, the whole poem can be found at the back of this book).

EXTENSION TASK 2:

Write an essay answering the following question: "To what extent do you find Victor Frankenstein a sympathetic character and his monster an unsympathetic one?"

NB. You may want to read the sections on the monster before starting the essay.

FRANKENSTEIN'S MONSTER

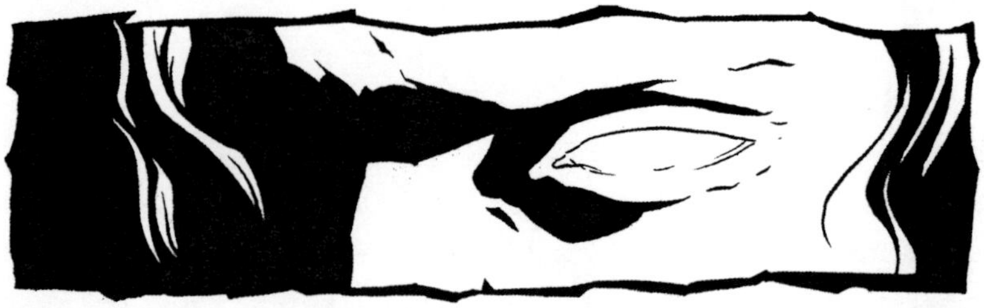

In cartoon and film versions of the novel the monster is often presented as a brainless semi-zombie, lumbering about in a stupefied manner. Actually, as you will have noticed, his character is rather complex, and when he tells his version of events we are encouraged to sympathize with him. Although technically he is the villain of the novel - the antagonist to Frankenstein's protagonist – he has many good, human qualities. For example the speed with which he learns to speak and then to read suggests considerable intelligence.

In her characterization of Frankenstein and the monster, Mary Shelley offers us something more morally complicated and rewarding than the simple goodie vs. baddie opposition of early gothic novels. In this she has again been influential. Think, for instance, of the presentation of Batman in recent films, where the caped crusader's "dark knight" side is emphasized.

QUESTIONS:

Write your answers on a separate sheet of paper.

1. How does the character of the monster develop over the course of the novel?

2. What events influence his development?

3. To what extent do you agree that the monster was originally good, but that experience made him a bitter and twisted character?

FRANKENSTEIN'S MONSTER

TASK 1:

From the list of adjectives pick the ones that you think best describe the monster.
Once you have done this, see if you can find an example from the novel showing each quality. The first one has been completed for you.

Adjective	Evidence
Intelligent	He quickly learns how to speak and then how to read, soon mastering difficult books.
Proud	
Strong-willed	
Cruel	
Loving	
Gentle	
Easy-going	
Independent	
Immature	
Considerate	
Confident	
Vain	
Kind	
Timid	
Greedy	
Heroic	
Brave	
Ambitious	
Weak	
Friendly	

QUESTIONS:

1. Are there any adjectives you would add to the list describing either character?
2. How many of the monster's qualities are the same as the ones you picked to describe Victor Frankenstein?

FRANKENSTEIN'S MONSTER

TASK 2:

A crucial turning point in the monster's development is when he saves the young peasant girl from drowning. Re-write this section from the point of view of either the girl or her father.

TASK 3:

In small groups see if you agree or disagree with the following points on the relationship between Frankenstein and his monster.

- Frankenstein was to blame for the monster turning to evil.
- The monster is mostly a sympathetic character.
- The monster loved Frankenstein.
- If Felix hadn't have driven the monster from the cottage in the woods, everything would have turned out differently.
- The reader sympathizes more with Frankenstein than with his monster.

FURTHER EXPLORATIONS

EXTENSION TASK 1:

The French Philosopher, Jean-Jacques Rousseau (1712-78), whose ideas had inspired the French Revolutionaries, disagreed completely with the notion of Original Sin. Rousseau argued that we are not all born "fallen" because of the sin of Adam and Eve, as the contemporary church taught, but that all people were born good and innocent. Furthermore Rousseau argued that society corrupted people; left to their own devices, in nature, people would naturally be good. Does this differ from Shelley's views as demonstrated by the life of the monster? Research Rousseau's arguments and list at least three key points that you would use in debate.
Point 1
Point 2
Point 3

FURTHER EXPLORATIONS

EXTENSION TASK 2:

Read the following poem by the Romantic poet William Blake.

The School Boy

I love to rise in a summer morn,
When the birds sing on every tree;
The distant huntsman winds his horn,
And the sky-lark sings with me.
O! what sweet company.
But to go to school in a summer morn,
O! it drives all joy away!
Under a cruel eye outworn,
The little ones spend the day,
In sighing and dismay.
Ah! then at times I drooping sit,
And spend many an anxious hour,
Nor in my book can I take delight,
Nor sit in learnings bower,
Worn thro' with the dreary shower.
How can the bird that is born for joy,
Sit in a cage and sing,
How can a child when fears annoy,
But droop his tender wing,
And forget his youthful spring.
O! father and mother, if buds are nip'd,
And blossoms blown away,
And if the tender plants are strip'd
Of their joy in the springing day,
By sorrow and cares dismay.
How shall the summer arise in joy.
Or the summer fruits appear.
Or how shall we gather what griefs destroy
Or bless the mellowing year,
When the blasts of winter appear.

QUESTION:

What, if any, connections can you see between this poem and Shelley's novel? Write your answer on a separate sheet of paper, if necessary.

EXTENSION TASK 3:

Do you agree with Rousseau that people are born good and learn to be bad from society? Get into small groups and debate this idea, using key points from the previous task.

ELIZABETH AND HENRY CLERVAL

Both of these characters are important in terms of plot, themes and characterization. Although neither Elizabeth nor Henry is especially interesting in themselves, they help to reveal the more human and sympathetic side of Frankenstein's personality. If two such good, decent people love him, he can't be all bad, we might think.

Both characters are presented as thoroughly likeable, constant companions. Even in the face of Frankenstein's peculiar behavior, and the long stretches of time when he fails to stay in contact with them, they remain faithful friends. Both, of course, are also the victims of the monster and each murder spurs Frankenstein and the plot onwards.

QUESTIONS:

1. To what extent do you find Elizabeth a sympathetic and believable character? Is she a stereotypically weak female?

2. *Frankenstein* was written nearly two hundred years ago. Since then society has changed in many ways. How might Shelley's novel be different if she had written it recently? If you have seen, or are allowed to see, the Kenneth Branagh 1994 film version, which is a 15 certificate, how closely does the film presentation of Elizabeth stick to the novel? What, if any, changes are made?

3. Henry Clerval is Frankenstein's best and only male friend. When Frankenstein is ill, or depressed, Henry is on hand to help him recover. Think of your own friends. Do you agree with the monster that a life without companions is a miserable one? Why?

WALTON

Walton is an adventurer and also the novel's first and last narrator. In many ways he has a similar character to Frankenstein; he is brave and adventurous and he seeks fame, even if it comes at the cost of his own life. Is his story necessary to the novel though?

QUESTIONS:

Write your answers on a separate sheet of paper.

1. Why do you think Shelley included Walton in the novel?
2. What would have been lost if the novel began at chapter one, with Frankenstein's story?

TASK 1:

Use the Internet and your school library to investigate other polar explorers and their expeditions. Two extraordinary people you may want to start with are Ernest Shackleton (1874-1922), especially his "Endurance Expedition" and "Scott of the Antarctic" (1868-1912). Either present your findings orally or in the form of a poster. If you are 15 or over you may want to watch another Kenneth Branagh film, the fascinating "Shackleton".

QUESTION:

Write your answer on a separate sheet of paper.

1. Judging from your research do you think Walton's character is typical of an explorer?

CHARACTER RELATIONSHIPS

TASK:

Draw a Venn diagram (a drawing, in which circular areas represent groups of items sharing common properties), of the character traits of Frankenstein, the monster and Henry Clerval and the relationships between them. Put the name of each character in three overlapping circles, with descriptions of their personalities inside these.

FURTHER EXPLORATIONS

EXTENSION TASK 1:

To what extent do you agree that Frankenstein's mother, Caroline, and Elizabeth are stereotypical female characters?

OTHER MINOR CHARACTERS

- Frankenstein's parents, Caroline and Alphonse.
- Justine.
- William.
- Felix, Safie and the De Laceys.
- Professor's Krempe and Waldman.

TASK 1:

Below is an example of a mind map. Present all the characters in the novel and their relationships in the form of a mind map. Use one of the images from the book in the center of the page to start you off.

Now draw lines to each character showing who is related to whom, how they are connected in other ways and any other "joining" threads you can think of.

Explain the connections, using quotes where you can.

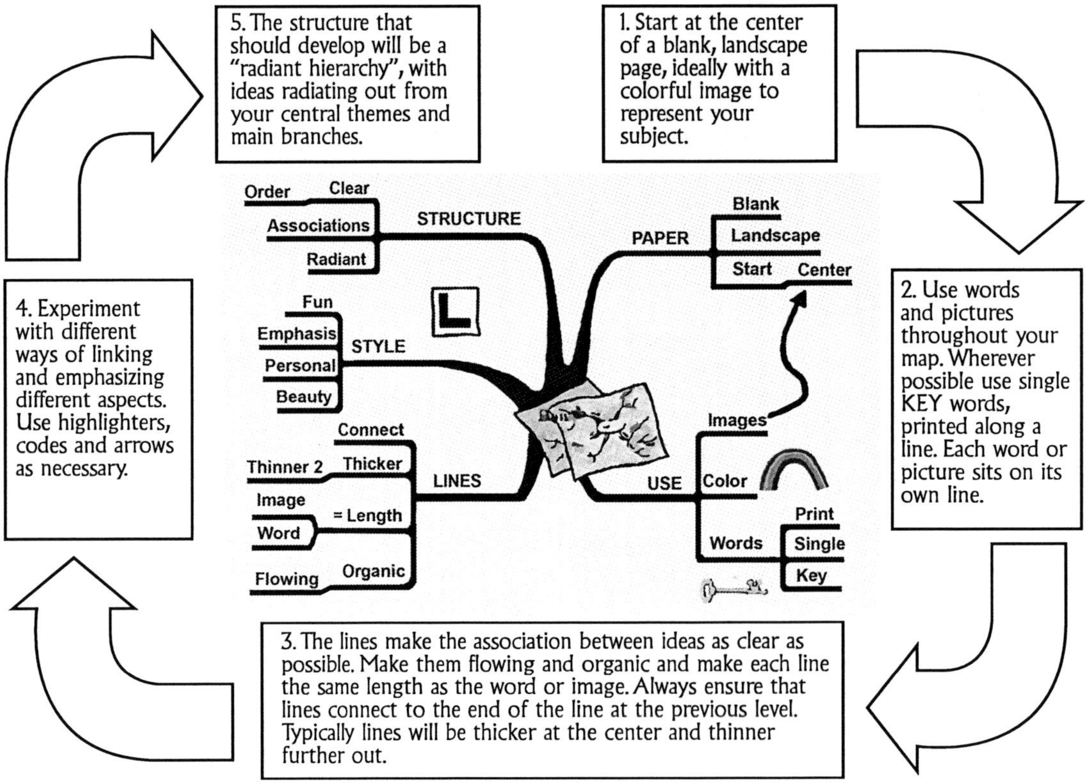

TASK 2:

Imagine the characters are pieces on a chessboard. Working in pairs, decide which characters would be the king, the queen, the knight and so forth. Compare your findings with other pairs.

TASK 3:

Working in pairs or groups, design a set of Top Trumps cards for the characters in the book. Decide what you will base the points ratings on.

OTHER MINOR CHARACTERS

TASK 4:

You may perhaps have seen the "Lonely Hearts" or "Soulmates" sections in magazines, or newspapers. The "Lonely Hearts" is where people write a sort of advert about themselves inviting other people to write back and perhaps form a relationship. The typical text goes something like this:

Beautiful, adventurous, female, 33, adores sports, especially swimming and cycling, and reading, believes life isn't a dress rehearsal, WLTM male, 30-50, professional, honest, creative type, to light up her life. Please enclose photo.

The text tends to be short, and abbreviations such as WLTM (would like to meet) are used because people pay per word. Often the writers start with some key adjectives.

Your challenge is to write "Lonely Hearts" advertisements for the following characters: Frankenstein, his monster, Elizabeth, Henry Clerval and Walton. Compare your texts with others in your class.

Frankenstein	
Frankenstein's Monster	
Elizabeth	
Henry Clerval	
Walton	

TWENTY QUESTIONS GAME

GAME

How much do you know about the characters in *Frankenstein*?

RULES:

Photocopy and cut out the characters on the next page.

Work in pairs, taking turns to hold the characters and ask the questions.

You are allowed just 20 questions to establish the name of the character your partner is holding.
If you guess incorrectly, your opponent receives 50 bonus questions, so be careful!!

The winner is the person who can identify the character with the least questions.

TWENTY QUESTIONS GAME

Victor Frankenstein

Frankenstein's Monster

Elizabeth Lavenza

Robert Walton

The Ship's Master

The Ship's Lieutenant

Alphonse Frankenstein

Caroline Frankenstein

Ernest Frankenstein

William Frankenstein

Henry Clerval

Justine Moritz

Monsieur Krempe

Monsieur Waldman

Lawyer

Old Woman

Monsieur DeLacy

Agatha DeLacy

Felix DeLacy

Turkish Merchant

Safie

Mr. Kirwin

Fisherman

Genevan Judge

IN THEIR OWN WORDS

For each of the five main characters, Frankenstein, his monster, Henry, Elizabeth and Walton complete the following character questionnaires. Write your response in the first person, (I), as if you are that character. You'll need to use your imaginations to answer some of the questions but don't worry if you can't answer them all.

1. What is your name?
2. How old are you?
3. Where do you live?
4. Describe your appearance.
5. If you could choose only two words to describe your personality what would they be?
6. Would you prefer to be ugly and clever, or beautiful and stupid?
7. Who are your parents?
8. Who or what do you most love and hate in the world?
9. When were you unhappiest?
10. What is your greatest fear?
11. What do you most like and dislike about yourself?
12. What makes you sad?
13. If you could have a superpower what would it be?
14. To whom would you like to say sorry and why?
15. If you could change your past what would you do differently?
16. How would you like to be remembered?
17. What single thing would improve the quality of your life?
18. Tell us one thing life has taught you.
19. What was your greatest achievement?

SHELLEY'S LANGUAGE

At times, Mary Shelley's writing brings the scenes vividly to life. Vital to effective descriptive writing are the choices the writer makes about adjectives and verbs. For the writing to be effective these words need to be colorful and expressive, appealing to a range of senses.

TASK:

The following scene is from Volume three, chapter 3 where Frankenstein sees the monster watching him as he builds the female creature. Your task is to fill in the blanks with the best words you can think of.

"I trembled, and my heart ...... within me; when, on looking up, I saw, by the ...., the daemon at the casement. A .... grin .... his lips as he gazed on me, where I sat fulfilling the task which he had allotted to me. Yes, he had followed me in my travels; he had .... in forests, hid himself in caves, or taken ...... in wide and desert heaths; and he now came to mark my progress, and claim the fulfilment of my promise.

As I looked on him, his countenance expressed the utmost extent of ...... and treachery.

I thought with a sensation of .... on my promise of creating another like to him, and trembling with passion, ... to pieces the thing on which I was engaged. The wretch saw me destroy the creature on whose future existence he depended for happiness, and, with a .... despair and revenge, withdrew."

SHELLEY'S LANGUAGE 2

A GOTHIC LEXICON

TASK 1:

Individually, or as a class collect as many spooky, gothic words as you can and share them on a whiteboard. Here are a few to get you started: *entombed, eerie, decay,* a particular favourite of mine *crepuscular* (the fading light of dusk), *sinister.*

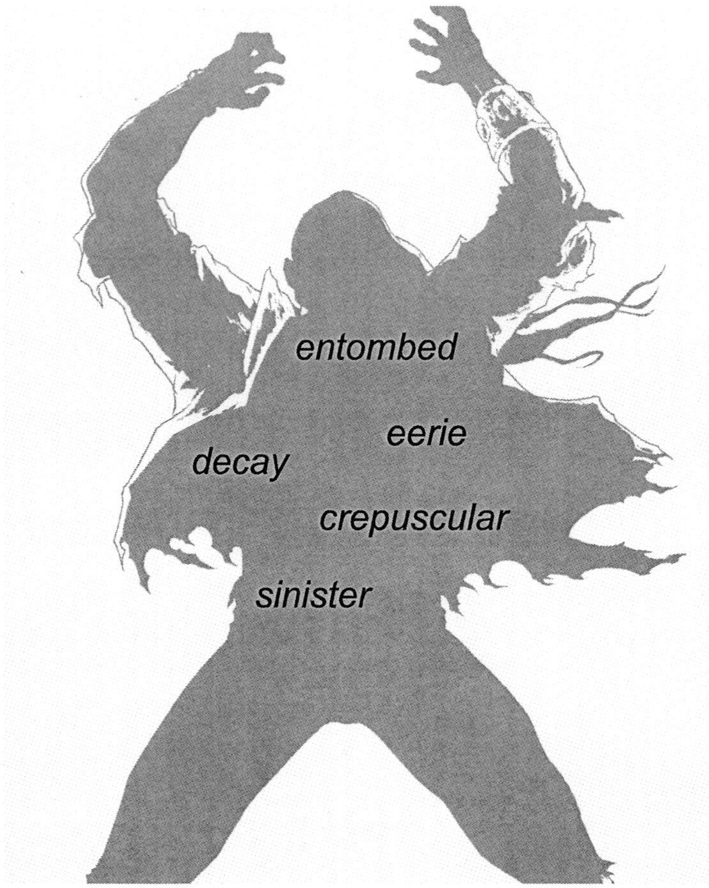

TASK 2:

Use gothic words to describe the picture on the right. Try to create as creepy an atmosphere as possible. Remember to use words that appeal to the reader's different senses and think too of near silence and stillness.

SHELLEY'S LANGUAGE 3

IMAGINING THE MONSTER

The familiar image of Frankenstein's monster, with its jagged black haircut and bolt through the neck is derived from film versions of the novel. In particular the 1931 film, by James Whale, with the famous actor Boris Karloff, has been influential in establishing this image as the definitive monster:

TASK 1:

Compare the descriptions from the novel with the above image. How similar are they?

- "a being which had the shape of a man but apparently gigantic stature".
- "The dissecting room and the slaughterhouse furnished my materials".
- "saw the dull yellow eye of the creature open; it breathed hard".
- "His yellow skin scarcely covered the work of muscles and arteries beneath; his hair was of a lustrous black, and flowing; his teeth of pearly whiteness; but these luxuriances only formed a more horrid contrast with his watery eyes, that seemed almost of the same color as the dun-white sockets in which they were set, his shrivelled complexion and straight lips".
- "A mummy again endued with animation could not be so hideous".
- "the deformity of its aspect, more hideous than belongs to humanity…the filthy daemon".
- "His face was concealed by long locks of ragged hair; but one vast hand was extended, in color and apparent texture like that of a mummy never did I behold a vision so horrible as his face, of such loathsome, yet appalling hideousness".

SHELLEY'S LANGUAGE 3

TASK 2:

Now compare these descriptions with the Classical Comics depiction of the monster.

QUESTIONS:

1. Which do you think is closer to the original?

2. Why?
   Write your answer on a separate sheet of paper, if necessary.

TASK 3:

Using only the information in Task 1, draw your own picture of Frankenstein's monster.

TASK 4:

In the novel we build up a picture of the monster through bits and pieces of description. As you can see from the descriptions quoted in Task 1, apart from the fourth example, Shelley generally avoids using precise concrete details. Instead she uses adjectives which communicate the emotional effect of someone seeing the monster. Picking these types of adjectives out of the examples quoted would give us, "filthy", "horrible", "loathsome", "appalling" and "hideous".

QUESTIONS:

Write your answers on a separate sheet of paper.

1. Why do you think Shelley has avoided giving the reader much specific description of the monster?

2. How (and why) does the monsters appearance change as we read the story?

CHECK YOUR UNDERSTANDING

MISSING WORDS

1. *Frankenstein* is a ...... novel.

2. In Ingolstadt, Victor sets out to discover the ...... of life.

3. Frankenstein's best friend is called ....

4. .... is blamed for the murder of William Frankenstein.

5. *Frankenstein* was written by .... Shelley in 18..

6. Walton is on an expedition to the .... to try to discover the secret of ....

7. When Frankenstein leaves the Orkney Island he is washed ashore in ....

8. The mountain range near Frankenstein's home in Geneva is called ... .

9. When the monster threatens Frankenstein, it says it will be with Victor on his ....

10. Henry Clerval dies by being ....

CHECK YOUR UNDERSTANDING 2

COMPREHENSION

TASK:

Read the start of chapter five, from Volume One and answer the questions which follow.

"It was on a dreary night of November that I beheld the accomplishment of my toils. With an anxiety that almost amounted to agony, I collected the instruments of life around me, that I might infuse a spark of being into the lifeless thing that lay at my feet. It was already one in the morning; the rain pattered dismally against the panes, and my candle was nearly burnt out, when, by the glimmer of the half-extinguished light, I saw the dull yellow eye of the creature open; it breathed hard, and a convulsive motion agitated its limbs".

"How can I describe my emotions at this catastrophe, or how delineate the wretch whom with such infinite pains and care I had endeavoured to form? His limbs were in proportion, and I had selected his features as beautiful. Beautiful! Great God! His yellow skin scarcely covered the work of muscles and arteries beneath; his hair was of a lustrous black, and flowing; his teeth of a pearly whiteness; but these luxuriances only formed a more horrid contrast with his watery eyes, that seemed almost of the same color as the dun-white sockets in which they were set, his shrivelled complexion and straight black lips".

"The different accidents of life are not so changeable as the feelings of human nature. I had worked hard for nearly two years, for the sole purpose of infusing life into an inanimate body. For this I had deprived myself of rest and health. I had desired it with an ardor that far exceeded moderation; but now that I had finished, the beauty of the dream vanished, and breathless horror and disgust filled my heart. Unable to endure the aspect of the being I had created, I rushed out of the room and continued a long time traversing my bedchamber, unable to compose my mind to sleep. At length lassitude succeeded to the tumult I had before endured, and I threw myself on the bed in my clothes, endeavoring to seek a few moments of forgetfulness".

"But it was in vain; I slept, indeed, but I was disturbed by the wildest dreams. I thought I saw Elizabeth, in the bloom of health, walking in the streets of Ingolstadt. Delighted and surprised, I embraced her, but as I imprinted the first kiss on her lips, they became livid with the hue of death; her features appeared to change, and I thought that I held the corpse of my dead mother in my arms; a shroud enveloped her form, and I saw the grave-worms crawling in the folds of the flannel. I started from my sleep with horror; a cold dew covered my forehead, my teeth chattered, and every limb became convulsed; when, by the dim and yellow light of the moon as it forced its way through the window shutters, I beheld the wretch -- the miserable monster whom I had created. He held up the curtain of the bed; and his eyes, if eyes they may be called, were fixed on me. His jaws opened, and he muttered some inarticulate sounds, while a grin wrinkled his cheeks. He might have spoken, but I did not hear; one hand was stretched out, seemingly to detain me, but I escaped and rushed downstairs. I took refuge in the courtyard belonging to the house which I inhabited, where I remained during the rest of the night, walking up and down in the greatest agitation, listening attentively, catching and fearing each sound as if it were to announce the approach of the demoniacal corpse to which I had so miserably given life".

CHECK YOUR UNDERSTANDING 2

QUESTIONS ON PARAGRAPH ONE

1.	In what month do these events take place? (1 mark)
2.	What is the weather like on this evening? (2 marks)
3.	Put Frankenstein's phrase "infuse a spark of being into the lifeless thing" into your own words. (2 marks)
4.	How does Shelley create a creepy atmosphere in the opening paragraph of chapter five? (5 marks)

QUESTIONS ON PARAGRAPH TWO

1.	Frankenstein chose some of the creature's features because they were "beautiful". Give two examples of these beautiful features. (2 marks)
2.	Some of the creature's features are ugly. Give two examples. (2 marks)
3.	Find a phrase from the passage to support the statement that it is not the ugly features in themselves that disgust Frankenstein but the combination of these with the beautiful ones. (1 mark)
4.	What techniques does Shelley use to make her writing vivid in this paragraph? (5 marks)

CHECK YOUR UNDERSTANDING 2

QUESTIONS ON THE WHOLE PASSAGE

1. What does Frankenstein first do when he realizes the "horror" of his creation? (1 mark)

2. Who does he see in his dream of walking the streets of Ingolstadt? (2 marks)

3. What makes the vision he sees in his dream so disturbing? (3 marks)

4. Frankenstein is horrified by his creation. Is his response the same as your own? Give reasons for your answer. (4 marks)

5. This chapter is one of the most celebrated in the whole novel. What techniques does Shelley use to make this extract effective? Consider the following and use quotations to support your ideas.
   - The use of setting.
   - The descriptions of Frankenstein's actions and emotions.
   - The images we are given of the monster.

   (10 marks)

CHECK YOUR UNDERSTANDING 3

TASK:

Below is a brief summary of Mary Shelley's novel. Unfortunately the order has been scrambled. Your task is to cut out the different phrases and rearrange the summary back into the correct order.

Frankenstein marries the lovely Elizabeth, but she is murdered by the monster on their wedding night.

The monster explains how it learnt to speak and read, and how it has suffered at the hands of man.

It admits killing William.

Frankenstein tells Walton about his family and his studies at the university in Ingolstadt.

Frankenstein pursues the monster to the North Pole in order to destroy it.

Meeting with the monster Frankenstein is made to hear the story of its life since he abandoned it.

Walton writes letters home telling of his meeting with Frankenstein.

In particular Frankenstein explains how he created his monster and then abandoned it.

Walton discovers the monster in the cabin where Frankenstein has died. It tells him it is going to kill itself. The monster leaps out of the window and is gone.

The monster promises to stop haunting Frankenstein, if he will build it a mate.

Having agreed to make a female monster, Frankenstein is suddenly revolted by his work and destroys it. The monster vows revenge.

Frankenstein hears that his brother, William, has been murdered.

THE IMPORTANCE OF SETTING

TASK 1:

There are a number of important settings in Shelley's novel. How many can you think of?

- Firstly, and lastly, there is Walton's ship and its location in the North Pole.
- Secondly there is Frankenstein's home, Geneva and the beautiful Alpine landscape.
- Next is Ingolstadt, the German University town, and within it Frankenstein's "workshop of filthy creation".
- Later Victor visits England and the wilderness of the Orkney Island.
- For the monster, there are also the woods and the hovel where he hides from humankind.

We're going to focus now on just two of the settings, Frankenstein's laboratory and the North Pole.

FRANKENSTEIN'S LABORATORY

"In a solitary chamber, or rather cell, at the top of the house, and separated from all the other apartments by a gallery and staircase, I kept my workshop of filthy creation; my eyeballs starting from their sockets in attending to the details of my employment".

"I collected the instruments of life around me, that I might infuse a spark of being into the lifeless things that lay at my feet the rain pattered dismally against the panes, and my candle was nearly burnt out".

Although in the novel Shelley does not give us a lot of specific detail about the laboratory, in film versions of *Frankenstein,* directors, or their set designers, often add lots of scientific equipment.

THE IMPORTANCE OF SETTING

TASK 2:

Imagine you have been employed as a set designer for a new film version of the novel. The director wants you to present your ideas for the design of Frankenstein's laboratory. Using the extracts on the previous page and any other information you wish, produce your set design. This should include:

- A sketch of the laboratory and its equipment.
- Ideas for lighting, including colors, textures and mood.
- A list of props, with illustrations of them, if possible.
- Any specific images you want to create.

You can either represent your ideas in pictures, in writing, or in a combination of the two.

Before you start you may want to do a little research on the role of set designers.

TASK 3:

Another important aspect in the successful transfer of the novel to the screen is the use of sound. To fully appreciate the significance of soundtrack watch a fast-paced scene or a spooky one from any film with the sound turned off.

The soundtrack can be split into two main aspects, the music, and what is called "ambient sound".

Ambient sound refers to all the noises of life going on around you that you can hear. Wherever you are stop and listen for a moment and write down the ambient sounds you can hear. From my room where I am writing this, I can hear cars running past the house every few seconds and the odd heavier rumble of a lorry; the noise of vacuuming coming from the living room; the wind in the trees outside, and the patter of my fingers lightly skimming over the keyboard.

Using the opening of Chapter Five, write down ideas for a soundtrack of this section of a film of *Frankenstein*. Start with the tick of the clock, nearing one, and the rain pattering on the window.

FURTHER EXPLORATIONS

EXTENSION TASK 1:

QUESTION: Write your answer on a separate sheet of paper.

1. Overall do you think Mary Shelley was criticizing or celebrating science in her novel? Give reasons for your answer.

THE IMPORTANCE OF SETTING

FURTHER EXPLORATIONS

EXTENSION TASK 2:

In Kenneth Branagh's version the director really goes to town, creating all sorts of extraordinary equipment: there is some kind of brass birthing chamber/coffin, from which the creature emerges covered in slime; there are chains and pulleys, wheels, harpoons and hundreds of electric eels.

The whole film is well worth watching, but it is 15 certificate. Either watch the scene in which the creature is born, or if you cannot watch the whole film, watch the film trailer. It's available online at www.imdb.com/title/tt0109836/

QUESTIONS:

Write your answers on a separate sheet of paper.

1. In what ways do you think the set design is effective?

2. How effectively does the director use sound to make the scene dramatic?

3 Apart from set design and soundtrack what other techniques are used to make the scene exciting?

In each setting where Frankenstein carries out his work he is isolated physically and mentally from any other characters, as well as from the natural world. His chamber is "solitary" and "separated" from other apartments. In the novel the ultimate place of isolation is, however, the North Pole.

THE IMPORTANCE OF SETTING

FURTHER EXPLORATIONS

THE NORTH POLE

Apart from Walton and his crew, the monster and Frankenstein, there appears to be nothing alive in this setting. This is the perfect place for the confrontation between the monster and its creator, because there is nothing else to distract them, as if all the rest of their lives have fallen away and become irrelevant. There is nothing in the white wilderness that is life-giving or life-sustaining. It is a place of desolation and of severe trial and potentially lethal. Symbolically, of course, all this emptyness could be there to suggest death.

Shelley's descriptions of this landscape make it seem immense and hostile to life.

- "The snow thickened, and the cold increased in a degree almost too severe to support".
- "(an) almost endless journey across mountainous ices of the ocean".
- "immense and rugged mountains of ice often barred up my passage".
- "I often heard the thunder of the ground sea, which threatened my destruction".

EXTENSION TASK 3:

Research the landscape of the North Pole.

QUESTIONS: Write your answers on a separate sheet of paper.

1. How effectively do you think Shelley uses the North Pole?
2. Was the North Pole a good choice of settings for the final battle between Frankenstein and his monster?

Mary Shelley acknowledged the important influence of the Romantic poet, Samuel Taylor Coleridge's nightmare poem *The Rime of the Ancient Mariner* on *Frankenstein.* As well as both texts sharing a similar idea about crime and punishment, Coleridge's evocative descriptions of the North Pole are echoed in Shelley's:

And now there came both mist and snow,
And it grew wondrous cold:
And ice, mast-high, came floating by,
As green as emerald.

The land of ice, and of fearful sounds
where no living thing was to be seen.
And through the drifts the snowy clifts
Did send a dismal sheen:

Nor shapes of men nor beasts we ken--
The ice was all between.
The ice was here, the ice was there,
The ice was all around:
It cracked and growled, and roared and howled,
Like noises in a swound!

(from Part III of *The Rime of the Ancient Mariner*)

EXTENSION TASK 4::

Research Coleridge's poem *The Rime of the Ancient Mariner*.

QUESTION: Write your answer on a separate sheet of paper.

1. Apart from the descriptions of arctic regions are there any other similarities between the two texts?

THE IMPORTANCE OF SETTING

Just as with the description of the horror of the monster, where it is the contrast of its ugly features with the beautiful that make it really disturbing, contrast is also essential in the novel's settings. Think about the laboratory and the North Pole and then consider the importance of Frankenstein's home and the surrounding beautiful landscape of the Alps.

QUESTION:

Write your answer on a separate sheet of paper.

1. What do you think that these places might symbolize?

TASK:

Now you are going to use the material you have produced so far to create a mind map of the settings in *Frankenstein*. Include all the settings mentioned at the start of this section: Walton's ship and the North Pole; Frankenstein's home, Geneva and the beautiful Alpine landscape; Ingolstadt, the wilderness of the Orkney Island; the woods and the hovel where the monster hides from humankind. Try to show what the settings symbolize and how they relate to each other.

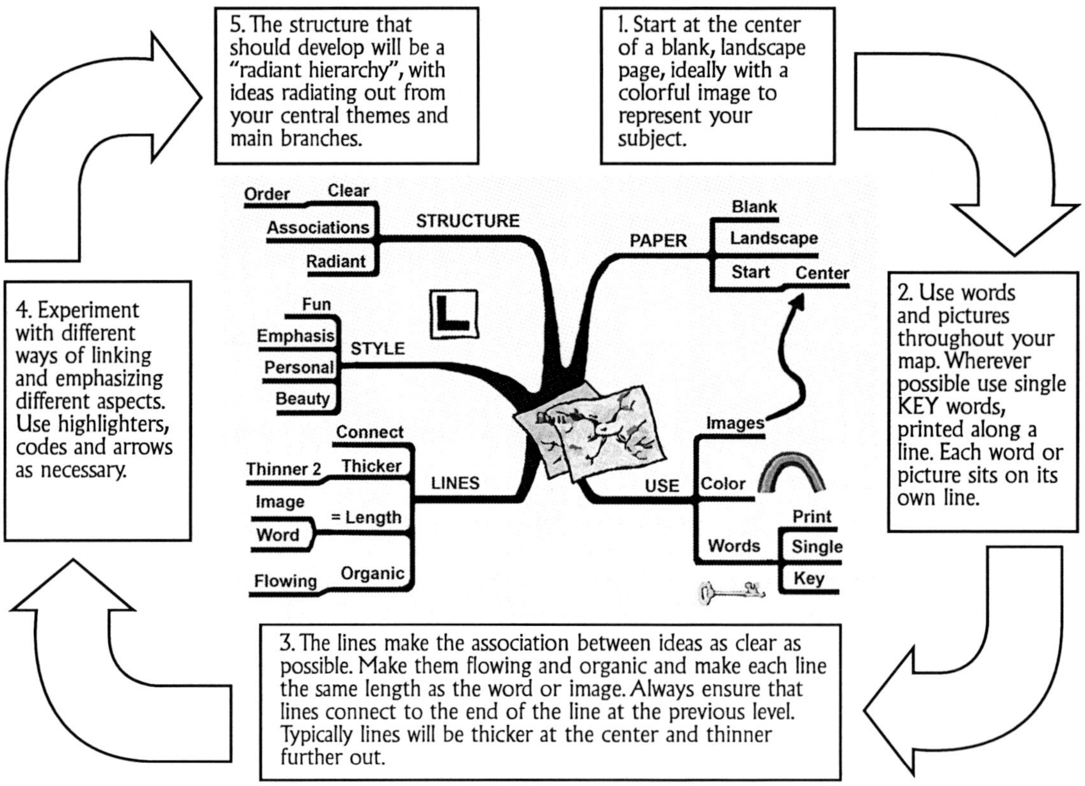

THE IMPORTANCE OF SETTING

REALISM AND THE GOTHIC

One of the potential difficulties of writing a gothic fantasy novel is that the events depicted may appear unrealistic and improbable. After all how often have you come across a ghost or a lumbering monster? Mary Shelley has a number of ways to deal with this problem and to make the events in the novel seem plausible: These are real settings; realistic characterization and the novel's narrative form.

REAL SETTINGS

As we have seen in the section on settings, a sense of place is important, particularly perhaps in a gothic novel. In early gothic novels, such as Walpole's *Castle of Otranto*, the setting is often a mythical, medieval past, far away from the society the writers lived in. A frequent feature of these settings is an immense medieval castle. According to Professor David Punter, an important critic of the gothic, in these novels,"The castle is gloomy, forbidding, a place where maidens find themselves persecuted by feudal barons, a reference to a medieval past which somehow remains as the site of our worst fears and terrors".

In contrast to Walpole and others, Mary Shelley sets her novel much closer to home. The action doesn't take place in some made-up world or country, but in Europe, in Switzerland, Germany, England and Ireland. Nor is the setting long, long ago. Instead Shelley sets her novel in her own time, in a world familiar to her first readers.

QUESTION: Write your answer on a separate sheet of paper.

1. What do you think might be the effect of bringing the gothic closer to home?

REALISTIC CHARACTERIZATION

Characterization is also very important. If we do not really believe in the characters then we are unlikely to believe in the events in which they take part. As discussed in the section on characterization, Shelley goes beyond simple stereotypes of "goodies and baddies", particularly in her presentation of the main character, or protagonist, Victor Frankenstein.

NARRATIVE FORM

By narrative form we mean Shelley's use of the first person point of view. Whereas Walpole and other early gothic writers tended to favor third person narration, (She did this, she did that) Shelley's choice means that we hear the voice of the main character, talking as if directly to us about events he has witnessed and taken part in:

> "His words had a strange effect on **me. I** compassionated him and sometimes felt a wish to console him; **but when** I looked upon him, when **I saw** the filthy mass that moved and talked, **my heart** sickened and **my feelings** were altered to those of horror and hatred."

This technique of first person narration creates a sense of intimacy between character and reader. Shelley's use of "real" non-fiction texts, specifically letters (a form known, technically as epistolary) enhances this sense of an actual person relating actual events.

THE NOVEL'S STRUCTURE

In *Frankenstein* Shelley employs what's called a "china box" structure. This means a structure where there are several layers of stories; one story is inside another one, inside another one, and so forth. Rather like a set of Russian dolls.

QUESTION:

Write your answer on a separate sheet of paper.

1. Can you think of how this "china box" structure fits Shelley's novel?

We have Walton's account of his adventures in the North Pole and his meeting with a "noble spirit", Victor Frankenstein. Inside this we have Victor's story of his creation of his monster and the exacting of its revenge. And inside this story we have the monster's story, which itself contains within it the story of Felix and Safie.

TASK 1:

Draw and label a diagram to illustrate the novel's structure. Don't forget to include the ending.

THE NOVEL'S STRUCTURE

CREATIVE WRITING:

In a modern story, email might take the place of letter writing. Write a short story about anything you like, written entirely in email, which follows Frankenstein's "china box" structure. Use the idea of forwarding an email to help you.

Another way of thinking about the narrative structure of the novel is in terms of peaks in tension and excitement. Traditionally in novels and films the level of tension at the start is low, as characters and a sense of place are established. Slowly the book or film builds to a climactic moment, where two people, or forces, or ideas, come into open conflict. Modern films and novels, however, want to start with a bit more of a bang and so often open with action scenes. A potential difficulty here, though, is that if this scene is too exciting then it may make the climax of the film disappointing.

Think, for example of the narrative structure of *The Lord of the Rings* or *Harry Potter* books and films and you'll get the idea.

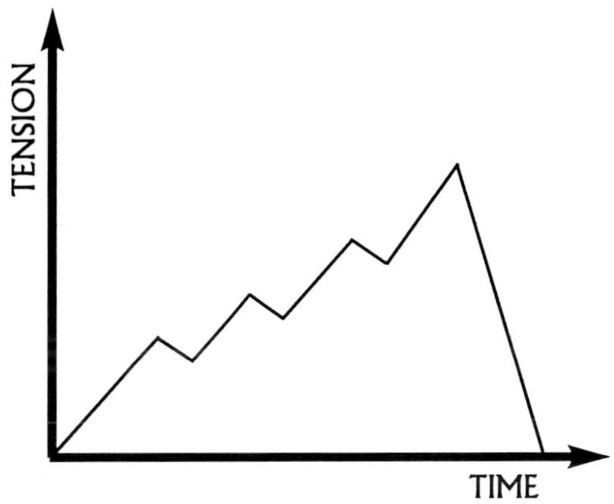

TASK 2:

Draw a graph with time in the story along the **x** axis, and tension level (scaled from 1 to 10) on the y axis. Now plot on the level of tension at various points in the novel. For example for chapter five, volume one, when the monster comes alive the tension level is going to be pretty high, maybe seven or eight, whereas tension will be low in the first chapter of the Frankenstein's story.

Label your diagram carefully to show where the peaks and troughs occur. For example:

- Everyone sitting talking, no danger: Tension = 0
- Distant threatening sounds: Tension = 1
- An argument or a flirtation: Tension = 3
- A fight, fire or passionate kiss: Tension = 5
- Murder or giving birth: Tension = 7
- Cold-blooded mass murder: Tension = 9
- Universe in danger: Tension = 10

SPEAKING AND LISTENING

CHECK YOUR UNDERSTANDING:

TASK 1:

You are going to hold a debate in your class about the moral choices we all have to make as a society about science. These moral issues are known as ethics. Using the statements below, half the class should prepare arguments to support one side, the other half prepares arguments to support the other side of the issue.

Statement 1

- It is essential that scientists are able to carry out their research without interference from anybody else.

Statement 2

- It is vital that scientific research is controlled by the government, public opinion, or other bodies.

Some research would be really helpful to make the quality of your discussion better than the one illustrated above. Recent debates about cloning, mixing genes and GM technology can be followed on reliable websites, such as the BBC and Guardian Unlimited site.

Once you have completed your individual preparation consult with other pupils preparing your side of the argument and choose one person to speak for you.

Someone, perhaps your teacher, should be moderator for this.

Let the debate commence!

QUESTIONS:

Write your answers on a separate sheet of paper.

1. Which statements on the next page did you agree and disagree on?

2. Can you come to an overall conclusion about your own feelings and thoughts about the ethics of science?

TASK 2:

Write up your debate in the form of either a discursive essay, or an article for a school magazine, aiming to inform your readers of some of the issues involved in scientific research.

SPEAKING AND LISTENING

CHECK YOUR UNDERSTANDING:

For each of the following statements decide whether you strongly agree, agree, don't know, disagree or strongly disagree and tick the appropriate box:

Statement	Strongly agree	Agree	Don't know	Disagree	Strongly disagree
A scientist should be able to research any area they want to.					
A scientist's research should be controlled by other people.					
Advances in science can be dangerous.					
Religion and science will always be in conflict.					
It is reasonable to carry out medical research on animals.					
Cloning of human beings may be a good thing.					
The aim to create AI (Artificial Intelligence) in machines is a good one.					
GM crops are dangerous, because we are tampering with nature.					
Mixing human and animal genes is immoral.					
There are some things that shouldn't be investigated by science.					

Once you have answered all the questions, compare your findings with a partner.

WHAT HAPPENS NEXT?

TASK 1:

Look closely at the pictures on each card in the following pages. In the box, write down what you think is happening in each scene. You need to have read the story first!

Comic Card	**WHAT IS HAPPENING?** Describe in your own words. Try to explain what is going on in each panel and what characters are saying. Can you remember what happens next?
CARD 1	
CARD 2	
CARD 3	
CARD 4	

COMIC CARD 1

Frankenstein Volume I Chapter IV

COMIC CARD 2

Frankenstein Volume II Chapter II

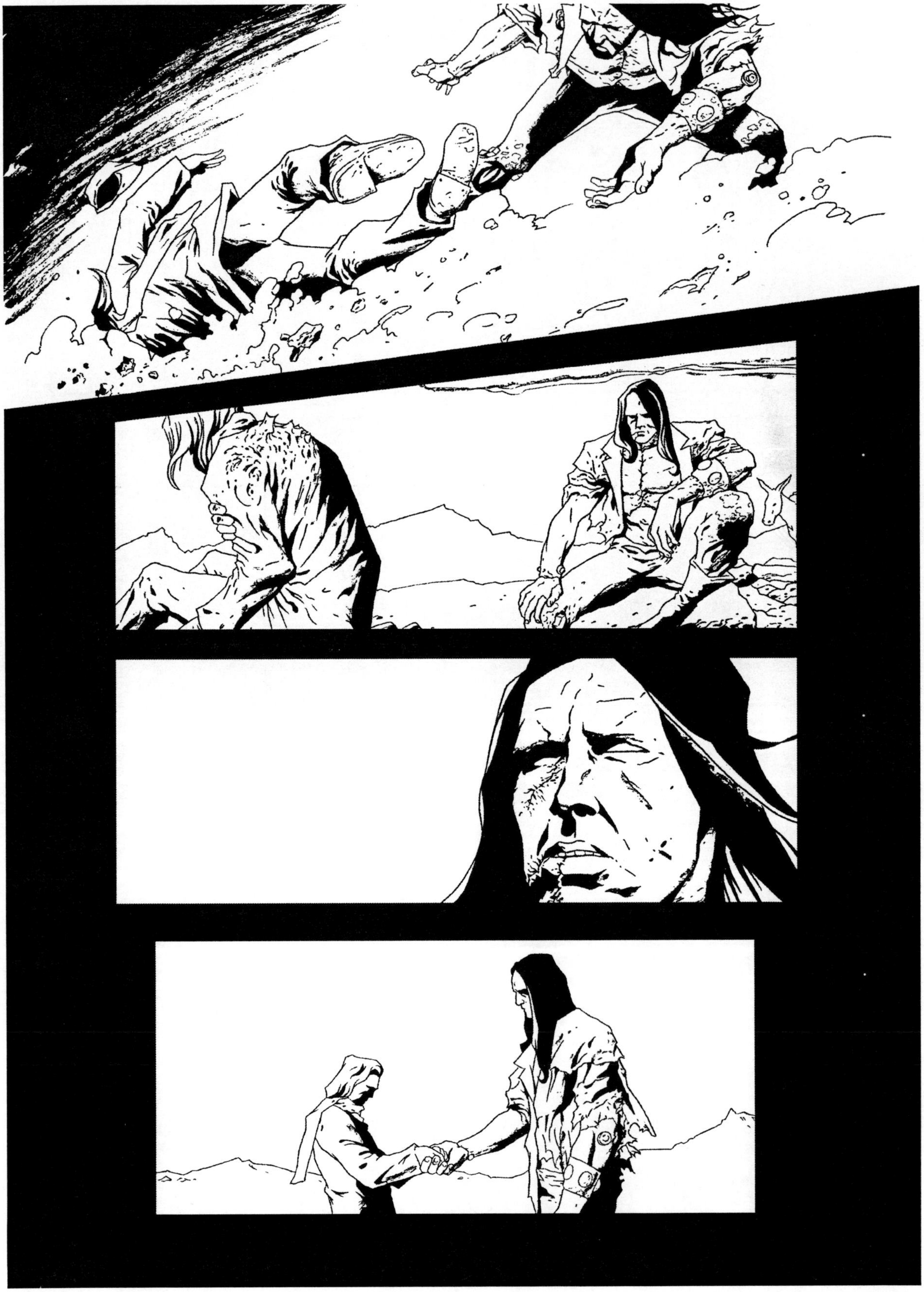

COMIC CARD 3

Frankenstein Volume III Chapter II & Chapter III

COMIC CARD 4

Frankenstein Volume III Chapter VII

WHAT HAPPENS NEXT?

TASK 2:

Look again at Comic Card 4. Cut out the blank word balloons below and write in them the words that you think that the characters are saying to each other.

You should:

- Make sure that the "tail" of the balloon is pointing at the correct character.
- Make sure that the word balloons follow from left to right so that you can follow the conversation easily.
- When you are sure that you have them in the right place, stick the word balloons to the sheet.

You could:

- Write the exact words from the play (this might be difficult to fit in!)
- Write the words in modern English.
- Make up your own words for the characters, but make sure that they are still saying the same sort of thing to each other.
- Write in what the characters are THINKING rather than saying.

There are more word balloons than you need here. You could draw your own if you prefer.

LITERARY INFLUENCES

THE PROMETHEUS MYTH

The subtitle of Mary Shelley's novel is *The Modern Prometheus*, which refers to the ancient Greek myth of Prometheus. The story is well worth reading, and can be found in many modern versions; what follows is a brief, simplified version:

Zeus, the King of the Gods, is quite content with his lot. He rules the world and the heavens and the unthinking, docile creatures called humans. Prometheus is a Titan, something between a God and a man and he feels sorry for humankind. He recognizes that in their dumb state, humans are no better than cattle, or slaves. Prometheus decides to rebel against Zeus, by giving humans a series of gifts. Brickwork, woodworking, telling the seasons by the stars, numbers, the alphabet (for remembering things), yoked oxen, carriages, saddles, mining,ships and sails were among those gifts, the most precious of which was the sacred fire stolen from Zeus.

The gift of divine fire unleashed a flood of inventiveness, one amazing result is that the humans wake up, become fully "alive" and start to think for themselves. In other words, Prometheus gives humans free-will and consciousness.

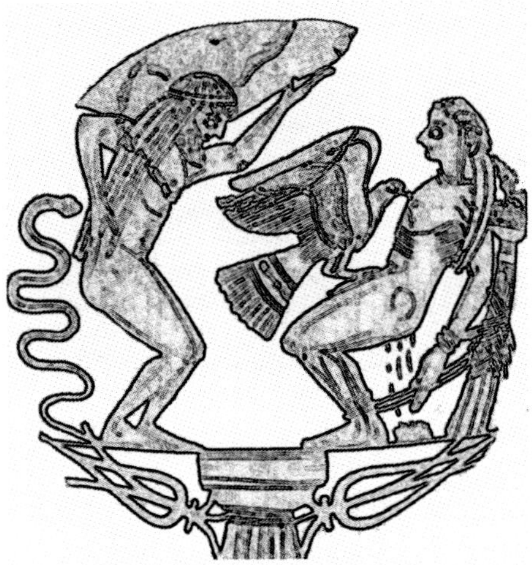

Zeus is not happy. In fact he is furious. He punishes Prometheus by having the Titan chained to the side of a mountain. Every day an enormous eagle flies by and everyday it pecks out Prometheus' liver. Although he is in agony, he is a Titan and cannot die. Instead he must suffer this punishment for all eternity.

This version of the myth exerted a powerful hold on the imagination of the Romantic poets and Mary Shelley's husband, Percy, in particular. He wrote a famous verse drama called *Prometheus Unbound*, in which he celebrated Prometheus as a symbol of liberation. But this Prometheus as liberator is only one of the versions.

The other later version of the myth shows Prometheus as a character who actually creates humankind out of clay. In this way he is seen as a less sympathetic character as he is no longer a liberator, but is aspiring to being a god.

QUESTIONS:

Write your answers on a separate sheet of paper.

1. In what ways can both versions of the Prometheus Myth be related to Mary Shelley's novel?

2. Can you think of another Greek Myth that can be related to *Frankenstein*?

LITERARY INFLUENCES

THE STORY OF BLUEBEARD

Bluebeard is a French fairy story written by Charles Perrault and first published in 1698. It tells the disturbing story of a young woman who marries a wealthy, but cruel aristocrat, called Bluebeard. Whereas the young woman is beautiful, the aristocrat is frightfully ugly because of his blue beard.

Not long after their wedding Bluebeard announces that he must leave his wife for a while. In the meantime she is to look after their grand chateau. Giving his wife the keys, Bluebeard issues a severe warning. The young woman is allowed to unlock the doors to all the rooms, except one. And under no circumstances is she to enter that secret room.

Once her horrible husband has left the young wife is overcome by curiosity. Come what may, she must know what is in the forbidden room. Taking the key from the ring she puts in the lock and turns slowly. The door creaks open.

If you want to know what happens next you'll have to look up the story! Be warned, though, it is all rather grisly.
A copy of the story is included in the back of this book.

CREATIVE WRITING

Either continue the story, making up your own ending, or, re-write any section of it in the first person voice of the young woman.

QUESTIONS:

Write your answers on a separate sheet of paper.

1. How is the story of Bluebeard connected to *Frankenstein* and the Prometheus myth?
2. Does the story of Bluebeard remind you of any other famous stories?
3. What do the Greek myths of Prometheus and of Pandora's box have in common with *the bible* story of Adam & Eve, our current book, *Frankenstein* and *Bluebeard*?

Other literary influences on Shelley's novel include *Paradise Lost* by John Milton. Milton's is an epic poem charting Satan's rebellion in heaven, his temptation of Adam and Eve and their consequent Fall. It was particularly influential on the Romantic poets because of its complex presentation of the relationship between the rebellious angel, Satan, and God.

As we have seen before, the Romantic poet, Samuel Taylor Coleridge's *The Rime of the Ancient Mariner* is another important influence. Mary Shelley includes a quote from this gothic inspired poem in *Frankenstein*. See if you can find out what this quotation is. Coleridge's description of a hideous, undead ghoul, called "Life-in-Death" might also remind us of a female version of Shelley's monster:

"Her lips were red, her looks were free,
Her locks were yellow as gold:
Her skin was as white as leprosy,
The Night-mare LIFE-IN-DEATH was she,
Who thicks man's blood with cold".

FRANKENSTEIN QUIZ

1.	What was the first name of Mary Shelley's husband?
2.	In what year was the novel first published?
3.	Where does Frankenstein go to University?
4.	What is the name of Frankenstein's best friend?
5.	From what materials does Frankenstein make his creature?
6.	Why does Frankenstein abandon his creature?
7.	What happens when the monster rescues a young girl from drowning?
8.	How does the monster learn to speak and read?
9.	The monster says it will stop haunting Frankenstein if he does one thing for it. What is this?
10.	What threat does the monster make when it discovers the female monster has been destroyed?
11.	Why did Frankenstein destroy the female monster?
12.	What does the monster do to avenge himself on Frankenstein?

FRANKENSTEIN QUIZ 2

1.	Whose letters relate the story of *Frankenstein*?
2.	To whom is this character writing?
3.	What is the name of Frankenstein's wife?
4.	What secret does Walton hope to discover in the North Pole?
5.	Who is Felix?
6.	What is the name of the character who is blamed for Frankenstein's brother, William's murder?
7.	Why is she blamed for the murder?
8.	How is the monster destroyed at the end of the novel?
9.	What is the novel's subtitle?
10.	Name one of the teachers at Ingolstadt University
11.	What prompted Mary Shelley to write the novel?
12.	How many volumes are there to the novel?

FRANKENSTEIN ANAGRAMS

See if you can solve the following anagrams. They are all either names of places or characters in or associated with the novel.

Jumbled Spelling	Correct Spelling
1. YAMR ELYLSHE	
2. NELYR EARVLCH	
3. GLOTISTAND	
4. UNITESJ	
5. VEGEAN	
6. HET SLAP	
7. DRLO YROBN	
8. XEFLI	
9. LOWANT	
10. HET THRON OLEP	

FRANKENSTEIN WORD SEARCH

Some of the following words appear more than once. How many times does each word appear?

VICTOR
FRANKENSTEIN
NOVEL
NIGHTMARE
GENEVA
GOTHIC
MONSTER
STUDENT
SHELLEY
WALTON
SCIENTIST
BYRON
NORTH POLE
THE CREATURE
WOLLSTONECRAFT

C N M E R A M T H G I N S S H E L L E Y
N Y N S N O M N I E T S N E K N A R F N
I E A N O R T H P O L E N O R Y B T S I
E L W T R O C I V E R A M T H G I N C E
T L A O Y B Y R O N C T N E D U T S I E
S E L V B N O V O L G T S B Y R O N E S
N H T I E T R E T S N O M H T O N R N O
E S O V C N O N O V E L T F E O C O T O
K T N I E R E T N O M C A H T L T S I T
N H V C C E T G L C I R N L I L L T S E
A E C T I T E H I H C G A R A C O E T E
R C A O H S N H T E S W O W E N O R Y B
F R H R T N T O N I G H T M A R E S N V
T E O L O O G O B Y R C I H T O G O R L
V A C T G M T S C I E N T I S T T E O L
I T I V C S N O R T H P O L E L T N T I
C U H H L I S S H E L L E Y A S H O C A
T R T L A V V E N E G V A W N I R R I R
O E O B Y R O N O R O B R O N N M Y V C
R W G T G R L E H N T T M T T G R B E O

FRANKENSTEIN WORD SEARCH 2

Some of the following words appear more than once. How many times does each word appear?

PERCY BYSSHE SHELLEY
LORD BYRON
VILLA DIODATI
INGOLSTADT
ARCTIC CIRCLE
MARY SHELLEY
FRANKENSTEIN
THE VAMPYRE
WILLIAM GODWIN
GENRE
LAKE GENEVA
ROMANTICISM
SWITZERLAND
ALBERTUS MAGNUS
SCIENCE FICTION
PROMETHEUS
FIEND
REVENGE
GOTHIC

```
E U S S O W N O R Y B D R O L L A K E G E N E V A H
G R W B C Y I Y M H N R M S I C I T N A M O R E L E
E S T I Y I S L D L O R D B Y E L A K E G E N E V A
N O U T L Y E N L I T S C I H T O G O V F E G R I M
R D O E L L E N E I B S C I E N C E F I C T I O N L
N G G H H I I L C N A G C W M L C E D L E S E R R F
E F I I F T N A L E O M O A H V E G N L E C C N D E
P R I A E R E O M E F R G T N N C N A A G E R P P M
R N Y N O I N M R G H I Y O H O I E L D N R Y V F C
O E I P D R M I O Y O S C B D I M V R I E N Y A T E
M E L E M V A A E R B D E T D W C E E O V E E D D O
E L R C T A D L V T P D W H I R I R Z D E G L N A I
T C O L R S V N B E S O R I H O O N T A R K L A T N
H R M E O I N E A E N N R O N S N L I T G I E L S R
E I A N G R C E H L R E E O L R Y D W I O R H R L E
U C N O I N D C K T R T G K M O O B S T M N S E O O
S C T I H R E B I N T E U E N A R M Y Y U E Y Z G S
O I I T H Y E V Y T A C Z S K A N D A C F G R T N T
D T C C O T E W E R C R I T M A R T B N R V A I I I
P C I I A R S Y R R O R F H I A L F I R I E M W E E
R R S F N P D N E I F N A S T W G C E C O C P S N A
O A M E I N G O L S T A D T N O S N I Y I N I O R Y
M O G C A F T D A T S L O G N I G I U H D S I S O E
E N S N F I E N I I E E G N E V E R E S O T M P M O
T N T E I E E E C I H T O G S G O T H I C G S R A U
H E Y I E N W I L L I A M G O D W I N I A E I O N G
E V W C N D T F L O R D B Y R O N E F L O E C M T E
U E R S L C O C N O R Y B D R O L E N H O S I E I E
S R E S A R C T I C C I R C L E C L O E C N T T C E
A V E N E G E K A L N I E T S N E K N A R F N H I S
L G V I L L A D I O D A T I E L C I H T O G A E S C
I G O T H I C T R E L C R I C C I T C R A D M U M M
V I L L A D I O D A T I C D L R U V E N G E O S C M
L A K E G E N E V A S S L O A R C T I C C I R C L E
W E I T E I M S I C I T N A M O R L O R D B Y R O N
Y L H T M E N H R Y G T N T L G R R G A H G I S E I
```

A POLICE INVESTIGATION

Imagine the end of the novel is different. Instead of Frankenstein dying on Walton's ship he is brought back to Geneva where he faces a trial. He is accused of robbing graves and perhaps even of committing several murders. By miraculous supernatural intervention you are able, if you wish, to interview dead characters, including Elizabeth and Henry Clerval.

TASK:

Split into two groups. One group will play the characters. If you are in this group you need to write a witness statement. This will include key information about your character, such as your name and occupation, your opinion and knowledge of Frankenstein and other gruesome events of the story.

The other group will form the police investigation panel. Your job is to write down searching questions for all the characters, so that the truth, like Frankenstein's monster, can be pieced together.

FRANKENSTEIN: A VERY ABRIDGED VERSION OF THE NOVEL!

TASK:

Working in small groups your task is to present a very short, but nevertheless comprehensive version of the novel *Frankenstein*. Your whole performance must last no more than five minutes. If possible record different groups' versions and compare them.

FRANKENSTEIN – THE SEQUEL

At the end of Mary Shelley's novel many questions are left unanswered and issues unresolved. For example, did Walton return safely from his journey or did he die on his Arctic expedition? Using his letters, has the whole story, in fact been pieced together by his sister Margaret?

Moreover who knows whether the version of events Frankenstein told Walton were fair and accurate? How do we know he was telling the whole truth?

And in the final paragraph of the novel we see the monster springing from the cabin window to be borne away on his "ice-raft" into the "darkness and distance". How do we know if he does actually build a funeral pyre and fling himself onto it?

The novel's "open-endedness", combined with the extraordinary popularity of the story, has inspired many re-imaginings and continuations. Sometimes these have been in a similar horror setting, such as *Bride of Frankenstein* (from 1935), and at other times the monster has been re-animated in comic settings, such as the 1960's gothic sitcom, "The Munsters". Other spin-offs from the original novel include, *Frankenstein Reborn*, *Terror of Frankenstein* and even *Frankenstein meets the Wolfman*.

TASK 1:

Make up some titles for potential film sequels to *Frankenstein.* Make them as believable, or improbable as you like, but make them sound worth watching. *Frankenstein II: The Vengeance of God,* for example, sounds better than *Frankenstein II: Here We Go Again.*

TASK 2:

As you will know, the "blurb" is the short text on the back of a book or DVD. The point of the "blurb" is to sell the film/book to you by making it sounds exciting. In other words it is a persuasive piece. Study the blurb on any book or DVD and analyze how it tries to persuade you to read or watch. Now write your own blurb for either the original novel, *Frankenstein* or for one of your potential sequels.

TASK 3:

Imagine that Shelley wrote one more chapter at the end of the novel. Write this extra chapter. Use this experience to help to answer the following question: How effective is the way Shelley ends the novel?

TASK 4:

Working in small groups plan a sequel to the novel in which **either** a character discovers Frankenstein's research papers and decides to build a new race of monsters, **or** Frankenstein's monster does not kill itself but lives on. Present your ideas to your class.

CREATIVE RESPONSES

1. Re-write chapter three, volume 3 *"I tore to pieces the thing on which I had been engaged"* from the point of view of the monster.

2. Imagine Frankenstein completed the female monster
   - Now imagine this creature "waking-up" for the first time in Frankenstein's laboratory. Using either first person narration (from the point of view of the female monster) or third person, write this scene.
   - The female monster is never described in the novel. Describe what it looks like and/or draw a picture of it.

3. Imagine you are a member of the Ingolstadt police and have been spying on Frankenstein. Write a report about his visits to graveyards and slaughter houses.

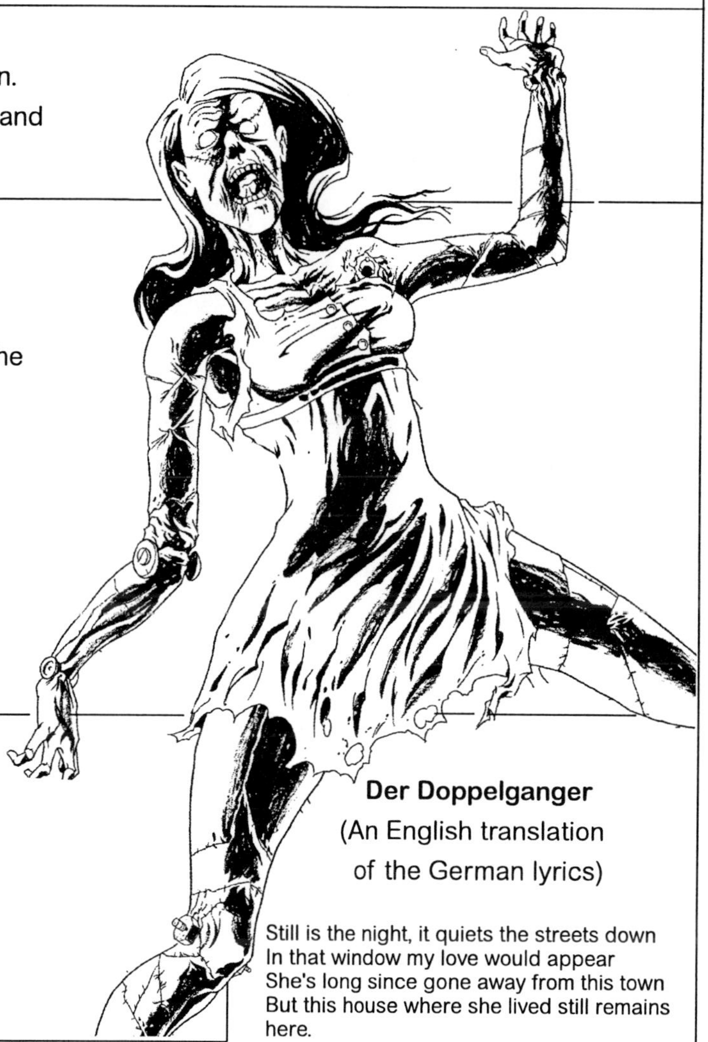

4. One of the most powerful images in the novel comes from Frankenstein's uneasy dream, after he flees from the monster. This dream features Elizabeth transforming into the corpse of Victor's mother.

   Find two images from magazines, one of something or someone glamorous and beautiful, the other of something or someone ugly. Using the images as a stimulus, write a transformation scene.

5. If you are allowed, watch all of Branagh's film of the novel. Apart from those mentioned already in this pack, how is the film different from the novel?
   Why do you think the director made some .. of these changes?

6. Listen to "Der Doppelganger" by the Austrian composer Schubert.
   Now look up the word "doppelganger".
   Can you relate this word and Schubert's song to Mary Shelley's novel?
   If so, how?

Der Doppelganger
(An English translation of the German lyrics)

Still is the night, it quiets the streets down
In that window my love would appear
She's long since gone away from this town
But this house where she lived still remains here.

A man stands here too, staring up into space
And wrings his hands with the strength of his pain
It chills me, when I behold his pale face
For the moon shows me my own features again!

You spirit double, you specter with my face
Why do you mock my love-pain so
That tortured me here, here in this place
So many nights, so long ago?

WRITING A LITERATURE ESSAY

Key aspects of a successful literature essay are the use of **analytical paragraphs** and the **ordering of your points in a clear structure.**

Analytical paragraphs are ones in which there is a clear point, usually established in the opening sentence, followed by some evidence from the text to support the point. The final element in this three-part, or tripartite structure is analysis of the evidence.

Analysis is different from description, because it requires you to explain the purpose and effect of writers' choices of language. As soon as an examiner reads phrases such as "the writer uses this word because..." they know they are marking a good response, in which things are being explained.

Remember: **PEA**

Point
Evidence
Analysis

Compare the following examples from essays by pupils.

1. "Frankenstein makes the monster in his laboratory and then thinks it is disgusting so he flees from it. Unfortunately for him he then has a horrible dream about Elizabeth and his dead mother. Then the monster follows him and Frankenstein ends up sleeping in a sort of shed".

2. "Frankenstein is also not a great heroic character because he is drawn "to the dark side". He researches black magic and occult figures, such as Agrippa, and in his experiments he aspires to being like God. Even Frankenstein realizes later that what he was doing was wrong, as he refers to his laboratory as his "workshop of filthy creation". The word "filthy" shows that he knows what he was doing was disgusting and immoral".

I am sure you will be able to recognize why the second example is better than the first. In number one the pupil basically re-tells the story and there is little indication of what question they are answering. In contrast, the second response follows PEA pretty closely.

Ordering your points

Before starting your essay, think of all the points you want to make. For this essay, which is about how much sympathy the reader has for Frankenstein and his monster, you might want to make points about the following:

- Ways in which Frankenstein is an admirable character.
- Negative aspects of Frankenstein's character.
- Frankenstein's treatment of his family and the monster.
- Negative aspects of the monster's character.
- Ways in which the monster is an admirable character.

Hopefully you can see that each of these points could be expanded into a paragraph, and that if you add an introduction and a conclusion, you will have a neat essay structure. In this case your structure will be mirror-shaped, and therefore appropriate to a question about Frankenstein and the monster.

DRAMA ACTIVITY

Victor Frankenstein wrestles with a number of dilemmas in the novel, such as whether to build the female monster.

TASK:

In groups of four either dramatize this scene or devise your own, one where a character faces a difficult choice.

For example, a pupil is being pressurized by his friend to play truant, but he doesn't want to do it. One of you could play the pupil, another his friend. The other characters could be a parent, or a teacher, other friends, or the "voice" of conscience.

CREATIVE WRITING

TASK:

Imagine you are one of the natives of the Orkney Island, where Frankenstein is building the female monster. You have grown very curious about what this strange man is doing in that old cottage. You've noticed that Victor goes out walking around the island in the middle of the night. Waiting for him to leave, carrying your lantern before you, carefully, anxiously, you enter his cottage and then, breathlessly, his laboratory.

Starting your story with watching the cottage, describe what you see, think and feel. Perhaps you could end the story when you are alarmed to hear the sound of footsteps approaching the cottage.

BOOK REPORT

A book report summarizes the content of a book.
Write a book report about *Frankenstein.*

Name: ______________________________

Date: ______________________________

Book Title: ______________________________
Author: ______________________________
Artwork: ______________________________
Publisher: ______________________________
ISBN: ______________________________
No of Pages: ______________________________

Characters: Who were the main characters?

Setting: Where and when was the book set?

Plot: What happens in the book?

Did you like or dislike the book? Explain why.

What new words or facts did you learn?

Ending: What happens at the end?

BOOK REVIEW

A book review is more detailed than a book report and assesses the book's strengths and weaknesses. When writing your review of *Frankenstein* think about these: Did you find the book interesting?
Did the format of the book help you to understand what was happening?
What was your reaction to the story?
Did you learn anything?
What would you have done differently to Mary Shelley?
Would you recommend this book to others?
Continue on a separate sheet if you need to.

Book Title: ______________________
Author: ______________________
Artwork: ______________________
Publisher: ______________________
ISBN: ______________________
No of Pages: ______________________

Once your book review is finished, you could upload it to one of the many book review websites such as:
www.amazon.com
www.whosreadit.com
www.kidsreview.org.uk
www.mrsmad.com
www.teensreadtoo.com

Book Review: ______________________

Name: ______________________
Date: ______________________

LINKS AND ACTIVITIES

Go online or use reference books to find out more and answer the questions.

What happened in the year 1816? (Apart from Mary Shelley writing *Frankenstein*!!)
Do you think these events influenced Mary Shelley?
How?
Who were Mary Shelley's famous parents?
What can you find out about Percy Bysshe Shelley?
Which other famous poet was with Mary Shelley when she started to write *Frankenstein*?
How many films have been made about the *Frankenstein* story?
Draw your own version of the monsters mate that Victor created and then destroyed.
On paper or on a computer draw a map of Europe showing all of the places named in *Frankenstein*.
Does Mary Shelley have any descendants living today? Trace the family trees and find out.
How does Percy Bysshe Shelley die, and where is he buried? Write a short story about his death and burial.

LINKS AND ACTIVITIES

Obviously you will want to check these sites and check their suitability for your pupils!

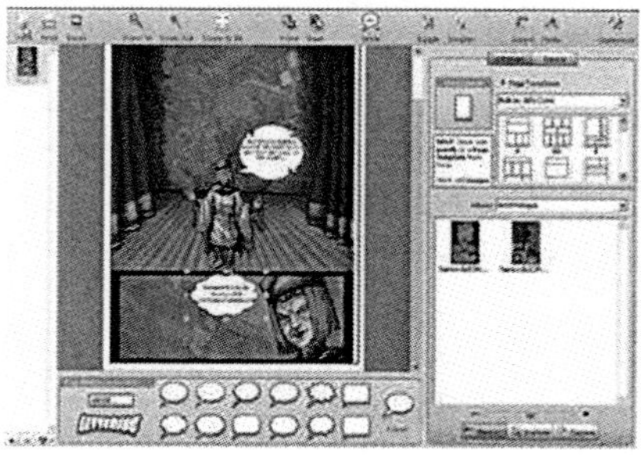

Design a graphic novel

Visit Comic Life and let your pupils create their own graphic novels – or re-write this one!

http://plasq.com/comiclife

On Mary Shelley's life and times

www.rc.umd.edu/reference/chronologies/mschronology/chrono.html

http://en.wikipedia.org/wiki/Mary_Shelley

www.victorianweb.org/previctorian/mshelley/bio.html

www.english.upenn.edu/Projects/knarf/Indexes/timeline.html#1816

Related sites

Frankenstein Films

www.wsu.edu/~delahoyd/frankenstein.films.html

An Early Review of Frankenstein

http://users.dickinson.edu/~nicholsa/Romnat/frankreview.htm

Presumption; or, The Fate of Frankenstein

www.rc.umd.edu/editions/peake/apparatus/drama.html

COLOR ME IN

COLOR ME IN 2

FRANKENSTEIN AND THE GOTHIC NOVEL
TEACHERS' VERSION

ANSWER: (PAGE 9) The answer is in **bold** below.

3. How are gothic novels different from horror?
There is no clear dividing line between the two. Broadly speaking, however, gothic novels are more psychological and creepy than horror. Often there is lots of blood and gore in works of horror, whereas gothic is more restrained. Where horror writers create excitement through violent action, gothic writers tend to seek to create suspense. And where works of horror aim to make the reader horrified or disgusted, gothic aims to create terror.

WHO OR WHAT IS THE MONSTER?
TEACHERS' VERSION

ANSWER: (PAGE 10)

In what is called a "socio-historical reading" of the novel the monster is a nightmare vision of the people, turning from innocent desire for freedom into a vengeful violent mob. Or the monster is an image of revolution itself, potentially good, certainly powerful, but also potentially evil.

VICTOR FRANKENSTEIN
TEACHERS' VERSION

ANSWER: (PAGE 20) The answer is in **bold** below.

1. What does Frankenstein wish to discover when studying at Inglostadt?
Frankenstein hopes to discover the "elixir of life". His motives are mixed.

ANSWER: (PAGE 22) The answer is in **bold** below.

1. How well do you think Frankenstein treats Elizabeth and his family?
Frankenstein doesn't treat his family very well; he fails to stay in touch with them or show interest in their lives.

2. Frankenstein is often called an "over-reacher" by critics. This means he pushes things too far, and oversteps boundaries. At what point in the novel do you think Frankenstein oversteps the boundary between right and wrong?
Probably once Frankenstein begins to collect "material" for his monster.

3. In some ways the monster and Frankenstein are similar characters. Both are isolated from their fellow men, both are very intelligent and both become driven by revenge. Why do you think Mary Shelley may have wanted her protagonist and his adversary to have similarities?
Shelley wanted to show that humans can be monstrous and monsters can be humane.

FRANKENSTEIN'S MONSTER
TEACHERS' VERSION

ANSWER: (PAGE 24)
The answer is in **bold** below.

1. How does the character of the monster develop over the course of the novel?
The monster develops from being good and innocent into being malign and destructive.

2. What events influence his development?
The key events are:
- **Being run out of town.**
- **Frankenstein's abandonment of his monster.**
- **Being shot at by the father of a girl he rescued from drowning.**
- **The kindness and goodness of Felix and his family.**
- **The monster's rejection by Felix.**

FURTHER EXPLORATIONS

EXTENSION TASK 2 (PAGE 28)

ANSWER:
The answer is in **bold** below.

What, if any, connections can you see between this poem and Shelley's novel?

The clear connections between Blake's poem and the novel are two shared ideas: One that we are born innocent, and two that experience can corrupt this innocence.

ELIZABETH AND HENRY CLERVAL
TEACHERS' VERSION

ANSWER: (PAGE 29) The answer is in **bold** below.

1. To what extent do you find Elizabeth a sympathetic and believable character? Is she a stereotypically weak female?
   Yes, Elizabeth is rather stereotypical.

2. *Frankenstein* was written nearly two hundred years ago. Since then society has changed in many ways. How might Shelley's novel be different if she had written it recently? If you have seen, or are allowed to see, the Kenneth Branagh 1994 film version, which is a 15 certificate, how closely does the presentation of Elizabeth stick to the novel? What, if any, changes are made?
   Elizabeth may be a less weak character, more involved in the action.

WALTON
TEACHERS' VERSION

ANSWER: (PAGE 30) The answer is in **bold** below.

1. Why do you think Shelley included Walton in the novel?

2. What would have been lost if the novel began at chapter one, with Frankenstein's story?

Walton provides another male character with which to compare Frankenstein. Their similarities in character suggest Frankenstein is not just a one-off madman, but a representation of a type. He can thus be seen as more representational of his society and its values. The novel is also concerned with "doubles", and Walton forms a double with Frankenstein.

Without Walton we would not have this comparison. He also serves a useful purpose in terms of realism. His letters allow "non-fiction" texts into the novel, and as an apparently reliable witness he makes Frankenstein's story more believable.

SHELLEY'S LANGUAGE 1
TEACHERS' VERSION

At times, Mary Shelley's writing brings the scenes vividly to life. Vital to effective descriptive writing are the choices the writer makes about adjectives and verbs. For the writing to be effective these words need to be colorful and expressive, appealing to a range of senses.

ANSWER: (PAGE 37) The answer is in **bold** below.

The following scene is from Volume three, chapter 3 where Frankenstein sees the monster watching him as he builds the female creature. Your task is to fill in the blanks with the best words you can think of.

"I trembled, and my heart **failed** within me; when, on looking up, I saw, by the **light of the moon**, the daemon at the casement. A **ghastly** grin **wrinkled** his lips as he gazed on me, where I sat fulfilling the task which he had allotted to me. Yes, he had followed me in my travels; he had **loitered** in forests, hid himself in caves, or taken **refuge** in wide and desert heaths; and he now came to mark my progress, and claim the fulfilment of my promise.

As I looked on him, his countenance expressed the utmost extent of **madness** and treachery.

I thought with a sensation of **malice** on my promise of creating another like to him, and trembling with passion, **tore** to pieces the thing on which I was engaged. The wretch saw me destroy the creature on whose future existence he depended for happiness, and, with a **howl of devilish** despair and revenge, withdrew."

SHELLEY'S LANGUAGE 3
TEACHERS' VERSION

IMAGINING THE MONSTER (PAGE 39)

TASK 1: The answer is in **bold** below.

Compare the descriptions from the novel with the above image. How similar are they?

The image and the descriptions have very little in common.

SHELLEY'S LANGUAGE 3
TEACHERS' VERSION

TASK 4:

In the novel we build up a picture of the monster through bits and pieces of description. As you can see from the descriptions quoted in Task 1, apart from the fourth example, Shelley generally avoids using precise concrete details. Instead she uses adjectives which communicate the emotional effect of someone seeing the monster. Picking these types of adjectives out of the examples quoted would give us, "filthy", "horrible", "loathsome", "appalling" and "hideous".

ANSWER: (PAGE 40)

1. Why do you think Shelley has avoided giving the reader much specific description of the monster?
   The lack of specific detail leaves a gap for our own imaginations. What we each imagine will be scarier for us.

2. How (and why) does the monsters appearance change as we read the story?
   The monster starts to decompose. As the monster develops from being good and innocent into being malign and destructive, so his body starts to rot to demonstrate the change.

CHECK YOUR UNDERSTANDING 1
TEACHERS' VERSION

ANSWER: (PAGE 41)

The answers are in **bold** below.

1. *Frankenstein* is a **gothic** novel.

2. In Ingolstadt, Victor sets out to discover the **elixir** of life.

3. Frankenstein's best friend is called **Henry Clerval**.

4. **Justine** is blamed for the murder of William Frankenstein.

5. *Frankenstein* was written by **Mary** Shelley in 18**18**.

6. Walton is on an expedition to the **North Pole** to try to discover the secret of **magnetism**.

7. When Frankenstein leaves the Orkney Island he is washed ashore in **Ireland**.

8. The mountain range near Frankenstein's home in Geneva is called **The Alps**.

9. When the monster threatens Frankenstein, it says it will be with Victor on his **wedding night**.

10. Henry Clerval dies by being **strangled**.

CHECK YOUR UNDERSTANDING 2
TEACHERS' VERSION

ANSWERS ON PARAGRAPH ONE (PAGE 43) The answers are in **bold** below.

1. In what month do these events take place? (1 mark)

   November.

2. What is the weather like on this evening? (2 marks)

   Dreary, rainy, miserable.

3. Put Frankenstein's phrase "infuse a spark of being into the lifeless thing" into your own words. (2 marks)

   "brought to life", or something similar.

4. How does Shelley create a creepy atmosphere in the opening paragraph of chapter five? (5 marks)

   Good answers should include:
   - **use of the setting – maybe the technical term pathetic fallacy of gloomy weather.**
   - **the symbolism of darkness, half-light and the 'half-burnt candle' (light of reason, God, human spirit).**
   - **Frankenstein's feelings of "anxiety" and "agony".**
   - **the image of the corpse and its waking up at the end of the paragraph (a mini-climax and cliff hanger).**

   Exceptional answers may notice the story's narration from the point of view of the main character, in retrospective narrative mode.

ANSWERS ON PARAGRAPH TWO The answers are in **bold** below.

1. Frankenstein chose some of the creature's features because they were "beautiful". Give two examples of these beautiful features. (2 marks)

   Lustrous hair and pearly white teeth.

2. Some of the creature's features are ugly. Give two examples. (2 marks)

   Any two from: watery eyes, dun-white sockets (and eyes), yellow skin just covering the veins; shrivelled complexion, straight black lips.

3. Find a phrase from the passage to support the statement that it is not the ugly features in themselves that disgust Frankenstein but the combination of these with the beautiful ones. (1 mark)

   The phrase is "a horrid contrast".

4. What techniques does Shelley use to make her writing vivid in this paragraph? (5 marks)

   Shelley's techniques include:
   - **Detailed visual imagery, especially the use of colors associated with death and illness.**
   - **Contrast.**
   - **A heightened, excitable tone: Frankenstein is uncertain (shown by the question) and uses many exclamations.**
   - **Credit any other point that is supported well from the text.**

CHECK YOUR UNDERSTANDING 2
TEACHERS' VERSION

ANSWERS ON THE WHOLE PASSAGE (PAGE 44) The answers are in **bold** below.

1. What does Frankenstein first do when he realizes the "horror" of his creation? (1 mark)
When Frankenstein realizes the horror of his creation he flees from it.

2. Who does Frankenstein see in his dream of walking the streets of Ingolstadt? (2 marks)
In his dream Frankenstein sees Elizabeth transform into his mother.

3. What makes the vision Frankenstein sees in his dream so disturbing? (3 marks)
The vision Frankenstein sees in his dream is so disturbing because Elizabeth becomes his mother's corpse!

4. Frankenstein is horrified by his creation. Is his response the same as your own? Give reasons for your answer. (4 marks)
Hopefully we do not feel exactly the same as Frankenstein. We may feel some distance from him, because we know what he is doing is morally suspect. We may also feel some sympathy for the monster and the way it is immediately rejected by its creator.

5. This chapter is one of the most celebrated in the whole novel. What techniques does Shelley use to make this extract effective? (10 marks)
Award marks for useful quoting from the passage and for the quality of analysis on the material.
Setting:
- **Frankenstein's laboratory is isolated from the rest of human society and social norms. Extra marks for half extinguished light, and the time of one o'clock, moral darkness and separation from normal behavior.**
- **The weather - "dreary", and the "rain" which "pattered dismally" that creates a sense of foreboding of what is about to happen.**
  Extra marks for observing the symbolism of the moon and questionable sanity.

Frankenstein's actions and feelings:
- **Extremities of his feelings, such as "anxiety to... agony"**
- **His sudden disgust at the "horrid" "wretch" he has created**
- **His blasphemous and exclamatory language "Beautiful! Great God!"**
- **His "rushing" out of the laboratory and abandoning the creature**
- **His feverish nightmare**
- **A deduction from this information that Frankenstein's mental state is highly unstable. Extra marks for recognition that the first person perspective and insight into Frankenstein's feelings draws the reader into the experience.**

The description of the monster:
- **"the lifeless thing"**
- **"the dull yellow eye of the creature"**
- **"a convulsive motion agitated its limbs"**
- **And any part of the Shelley description: "His yellow skin ... and straight black lips." Extra marks for observing that the creature is unnatural – how it is like a human, but also unlike us.**

CHECK YOUR UNDERSTANDING 3
TEACHERS' VERSION

TASK: (PAGE 45)

ANSWER: The correct sequence for the summary of the novel is:

Walton writes letters home telling of his meeting with Frankenstein.

Frankenstein tells Walton about his family and his studies at the university in Ingolstadt.

In particular Frankenstein explains how he created his monster and then abandoned it.

Frankenstein hears that his brother, William, has been murdered.

Meeting with the monster, Frankenstein is made to hear the story of its life since he abandoned it.

The monster explains how it learnt to speak and read, and how it has suffered at the hands of man. It admits killing William.

The monster promises to stop haunting Frankenstein, if he will build it a mate.

Having agreed to make a female monster, Frankenstein is suddenly revolted by his work and destroys it. The monster vows revenge.

Frankenstein marries the lovely Elizabeth, but she is murdered by the monster on their wedding night.

Frankenstein pursues the monster to the North Pole in order to destroy it.

Walton discovers the monster in the cabin where Frankenstein has died. It tells him it is going to kill itself. The monster leaps out of the window and is gone.

THE IMPORTANCE OF SETTING
TEACHERS' VERSION

FURTHER EXPLORATIONS (PAGE 48)

EXTENSION TASK 2:

ANSWERS: 1, 2 & 3:

Good answers may refer to the quick editing of the scene and swift switches between different camera shots (bird's-eye-view, close-up, p.o.v. shot etc.). Lighting is also important, but may be incorporated in set design.

THE NORTH POLE (PAGE 49)

EXTENSION TASK 3:

Research the landscape of the North Pole.

ANSWER: The answer is in **bold** below.

1. How effectively do you think Shelley uses the North Pole?
2. Was the North Pole a good choice of settings for the final battle between Frankenstein and his monster?

   Yes. Give credit for any sensible reasoning.

EXTENSION TASK 4::

Research Coleridge's poem *The Rime of the Ancient Mariner.*

ANSWER: The answer is in **bold** below.

1. Apart from the descriptions of arctic regions are there any other similarities between the two texts?
   Yes, there are a number of similarities between the two texts. Here are just a few:
   - **The main characters being "cursed" and isolated by their experiences.**
   - **Their relation of their stories to another character (Walton and the wedding guest).**
   - **The idea of a crime against nature and consequent supernatural punishment.**
   - **The idea of beauty in nature as a potential curative and blessing.**

   The effect of bringing the gothic "closer to home" is probably to make it more disturbing and realistic.

WHAT HAPPENS NEXT?

TASK 1: (PAGE 56)

Teachers' Note

This is an activity that is primarily a reading activity disguised as art. The range of scenes covered by the cards home in on some of the key moments, encouraging the pupils to make connections between different parts of the text. A knowledge of the text will be needed to be able to complete the first task "What Happens Next?"

SUGGESTED ANSWERS:

Comic Card	**WHAT IS HAPPENING?** Describe in your own words. Try to explain what is going on in each panel and what characters are saying. Can you remember what happens next?
Comic Card 1	In **Volume I Chapter IV** After 2 years relentless hard work the monster is brought to life. Victor flees from his laboratory in fear and horror, only for the "wretch", the "demoniacal corpse" to follow him. **What happens next?** Abandoning the creature, Frankenstein spends the night wandering the dismal streets of Ingolstadt, where, by pure chance he meets his old friend Henry Clerval. The mixture of excitement and dread, coupled with physical exhaustion bring on a "nervous fever" and Frankenstein collapses. During several hard months Henry nurses his friend.
Comic Card 2	In **Volume II Chapter II** Two months pass and Frankenstein is despondent, tortured by guilt. He travels into one of the beautiful valleys of the Alps to find the monster. **What happens next?** The following day the weather becomes stormy and Frankenstein's mood also darkens. Nevertheless he continues to travel towards the monster. Frankenstein and the monster talk, and Victor is persuaded to visit the monster's hut to hear his story.
Comic Card 3	In **Volume III Chapter II & Chapter III** Frankenstein promises to begin constructing a female monster, as soon as he can. He journeys to a remote Orkney island. **What happens next?** There, alone, he begins his work. Frankenstein is appalled by the idea of releasing more evil into the world. He destroys the creature he has been making. The monster is watching him and warns Victor "I shall be with you on your wedding night".
Comic Card 4	In **Volume III Chapter VII** Walton takes up the story in letters. The ship is in terrible peril. "Surrounded by mountains of ice". Its crew demand they return at the first opportunity to England. Frankenstein, who is dying, asks Walton to complete his mission and kill the monster. **What happens next?** Frankenstein dies. Walton is disturbed by noises. He finds the monster kneeling over the body of its creator. The monster tells Walton of its wretchedness and suffering and plans to kill itself. The monster leaps out of the window and is soon "borne away, and lost in darkness and distance". And thus the novel ends.

KEY IDEAS
TEACHERS' VERSION

LITERARY INFLUENCES (PAGE 62)

THE PROMETHEUS MYTH

ANSWERS 1 & 2: The answer is in **bold** below.

1. In what ways can both versions of the Prometheus Myth be related to Mary Shelley's novel?
2. Can you think of another Greek Myth that can be related to *Frankenstein*?

The first story of Prometheus stealing divine fire shows Frankenstein in a favorable light as someone making a discovery that may benefit humankind. The second version relates to Frankenstein's "hubris", in Christian terms his sinful aspiration to Godhead. A clearly related Greek creation myth is *Pandora's Box*. *Orpheus and Eurydice* is also connected through the desire to defeat death, and the failure to follow a prohibition.

CREATIVE WRITING (PAGE 63)

ANSWERS 1-3: The answer is in **bold** below.

1. How is the story of Bluebeard connected to *Frankenstein* and the Prometheus myth?
2. Does the story of Bluebeard remind you of any other famous stories?
3. What do the Greek myths of Prometheus and of Pandora's Box have in common with *The Bible* story of Adam & Eve, *Frankenstein* and *Bluebeard*?

They are stories which deal with the idea of "forbidden knowledge" and the consequences of transgressing against a prohibition.

FRANKENSTEIN QUIZ
TEACHERS' VERSION

ANSWER: (PAGE 64) The answers are in **bold** below.

1. What was the first name of Mary Shelley's husband?

   Percy.

2. In what year was the novel first published?

   1818.

3. Where does Frankenstein go to University?

   Ingolstadt.

4. What is the name of Frankenstein's best friend?

   Henry Clerval.

5. From what materials does Frankenstein make his creature?

   Corpses.

6. Why does Frankenstein abandon his creature?

   Because it is hideous.

7. What happens when the monster rescues a young girl from drowning?

   Her father shoots him.

8. How does the monster learn to speak and read?

   By copying Felix and his family.

9. The monster says it will stop haunting Frankenstein if he does one thing for it. What is this?

   Make it a mate.

10. What threat does the monster make when it discovers the female monster has been destroyed?

    It will be with him on his wedding night.

11. Why did Frankenstein destroy the female monster?

    Because he fears creating a race of monsters.

12. What does the monster do to avenge himself on Frankenstein?

    Kills William, Clerval and Elizabeth.

FRANKENSTEIN QUIZ 2
TEACHERS' VERSION

ANSWER: (PAGE 65) The answers are in **bold** below.

1.	Whose letters relate the story of *Frankenstein*? **Walton.**
2.	To whom is this character writing? **To his sister, Margaret.**
3.	What is the name of Frankenstein's wife? **Elizabeth.**
4.	What secret does Walton hope to discover in the North Pole? **The secret of magnetism.**
5.	Who is Felix? **A young man, part of a family that the monster watches.**
6.	What is the name of the character who is blamed for Frankenstein's brother, William's murder? **Justine.**
7.	Why is she blamed for the murder? **She has a valuable pendant on her.**
8.	How is the monster destroyed at the end of the novel? **Trick question – we don't know.**
9.	What is the novel's subtitle? **"The Modern Prometheus"**
10.	Name one of the teachers at Ingolstadt University **Kempe & Waldman.**
11.	What prompted Mary Shelley to write the novel? **A competition set by Byron.**
12.	How many volumes are there to the novel? **Three.**

FRANKENSTEIN ANAGRAMS
TEACHERS' VERSION

ANSWER: (PAGE 66) The answers are in **bold** below.

See if you can solve the following anagrams. They are all either names of places or characters in or associated with the novel.

Jumbled Spelling	Correct Spelling
1. YAMR ELYLSHE	**Mary Shelley**
2. NELYR EARVLCH	**Henry Clerval**
3. GLOTISTAND	**Ingolstadt**
4. UNITESJ	**Justine**
5. VEGEAN	**Geneva**
6. HET SLAP	**The Alps**
7. DRLO YROBN	**Lord Byron**
8. XEFLI	**Felix**
9. LOWANT	**Walton**
10. HET THRON OLEP	**The North Pole**

FRANKENSTEIN WORD SEARCH
TEACHERS' VERSION

SOLUTION: (PAGE 67)

VICTOR (5)	GOTHIC (6)	SCIENTIST (2)
FRANKENSTEIN (2)	MONSTER (3)	BYRON (7)
NOVEL (2)	STUDENT	NORTH POLE
NIGHTMARE (3)	SHELLEY (4)	THE CREATURE
GENEVA	WALTON (4)	WOLLSTONECRAFT

C	N	M	E	R	A	M	T	H	G	I	N	S	S	H	E	L	L	E	Y
N	Y	N	S	N	O	M	N	I	E	T	S	N	E	K	N	A	R	F	N
I	E	A	N	O	R	T	H	P	O	L	E	N	O	R	Y	B	T	S	I
E	L	W	T	R	O	C	I	V	E	R	A	M	T	H	G	I	N	C	E
T	L	A	O	Y	B	Y	R	O	N	C	T	N	E	D	U	T	S	I	E
S	E	L	V	B	N	O	V	O	L	G	T	S	B	Y	R	O	N	E	S
N	H	T	I	E	T	R	E	T	S	N	O	M	H	T	O	N	R	N	O
E	S	O	V	C	N	O	N	O	V	E	L	T	F	E	O	C	O	T	O
K	T	N	I	E	R	E	T	N	O	M	C	A	H	T	L	T	S	I	T
N	H	V	C	C	E	T	G	L	C	I	R	N	L	I	L	L	T	S	E
A	E	C	T	I	T	E	H	I	H	C	G	A	R	A	C	O	E	T	E
R	C	A	O	H	S	N	H	T	E	S	W	O	W	E	N	O	R	Y	B
F	R	H	R	T	N	T	O	N	I	G	H	T	M	A	R	E	S	N	V
T	E	O	L	O	O	G	O	B	Y	R	C	I	H	T	O	G	O	R	L
V	A	C	T	G	M	T	S	C	I	E	N	T	I	S	T	T	E	O	L
I	T	I	V	C	S	N	O	R	T	H	P	O	L	E	L	T	N	T	I
C	U	H	H	L	I	S	S	H	E	L	L	E	Y	A	S	H	O	C	A
T	R	T	L	A	V	V	E	N	E	G	V	A	W	N	I	R	R	I	R
O	E	O	B	Y	R	O	N	O	R	O	B	R	O	N	N	M	Y	V	C
R	W	G	T	G	R	L	E	H	N	T	T	M	T	T	G	R	B	E	O

FRANKENSTEIN WORD SEARCH 2
TEACHERS' VERSION

SOLUTION: (PAGE 68)

PERCY BYSSHE SHELLEY
LORD BYRON
VILLA DIODATI
INGOLSTADT (3)
ARCTIC CIRCLE
MARY SHELLEY
FRANKENSTEIN (3)
THE VAMPYRE
WILLIAM GODWIN
GENRE (2)
LAKE GENEVA
ROMANTICISM (6)
SWITZERLAND (3)
ALBERTUS MAGNUS
SCIENCE FICTION
PROMETHEUS (4)
FIEND (4)
REVENGE (4)
GOTHIC (7)

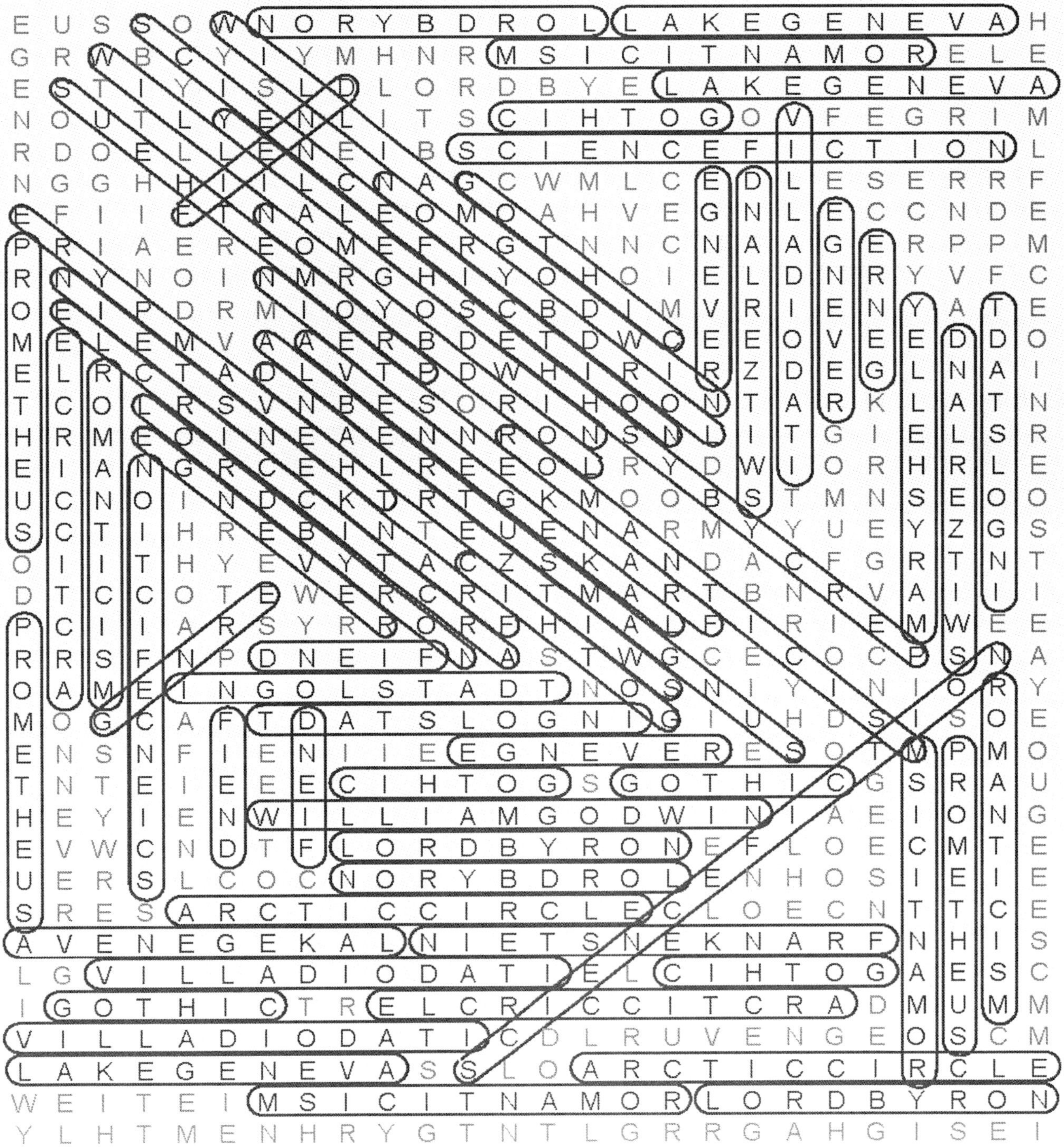

LINKS AND ACTIVITIES
TEACHERS' VERSION

ANSWERS: (PAGE 76)

Suggested web links and answers are in **bold** below.

What happened in the year 1816? (Apart from Mary Shelley writing *Frankenstein*!!) **The Year Without a Summer, also known as the Poverty Year, The Year There Was No Summer or Eighteen hundred and froze to death, was 1816, in which severe summer climate abnormalities destroyed crops in Northern Europe, the American Northeast and eastern Canada. http://en.wikipedia.org/wiki/Year_Without_a_Summer**
Do you think these events influenced Mary Shelley? **These events, almost certainly, did influence Mary Shelley.**
How? **Percy Shelley rented a smaller building called Maison Chapuis on the waterfront close to Lake Geneva at the village of Cologny; It was here Mary Shelley and her friends spent their time writing, boating on the lake, and talking late into the night. "It proved a wet, ungenial summer", Mary Shelley remembered in 1831, "and incessant rain often confined us for days to the house". The conversation turned to the experiments of the 18th-century natural philosopher and poet Erasmus Darwin,who was said to have animated dead matter, and to galvanism and the feasibility of returning a corpse or assembled body parts to life. http://en.wikipedia.org/wiki/Mary_Shelley**
Who were Mary Shelley's famous parents? **Mary Shelley was the daughter of William Godwin, the foremost English writer on the French Revolution and his wife Mary Wollstonecraft.**
What can you find out about Percy Bysshe Shelley? **Percy Bysshe Shelley (August 4, 1792 – July 8, 1822); was one of the major English Romantic poets and is widely considered to be among the finest lyric poets in the English language. He is perhaps most famous for such anthology pieces as** *Ozymandias*, *Ode to the West Wind*, *To a Skylark*, **and** *The Masque of Anarchy*. **http://en.wikipedia.org/wiki/Percy_Bysshe_Shelley**
Which other famous poet was with Mary Shelley when she started to write *Frankenstein*? **George Gordon Noel Byron, later 6th Baron Byron of Rochdale. http://www.encyclopedia.com/topic/George_Gordon_Noel_Byron_6th_Baron_Byron.aspx**
How many films have been made about the *Frankenstein* story? **See the two links listed to find out more. http://www.wsu.edu/~delahoyd/frankenstein.films.html http://en.wikipedia.org/wiki/Frankenstein_in_popular_culture**
Draw your own version of the monsters mate that Victor created and then destroyed.
On paper or on a computer draw a map of Europe showing all of the places named in *Frankenstein*.
Does Mary Shelley have any descendants living today? Trace the family trees and find out. **Mary Shelley's last descendent was her son Percy Florence, who died childless in 1889.**
How does Percy Bysshe Shelley die, and where is he buried? Write a short story about his death and burial. **On July 8, 1822, less than a month before his 30th birthday, Shelley drowned in a sudden storm while sailing back from Livorno to Lerici in his schooner, Don Juan. Shelley's body was washed ashore and later, in keeping with quarantine regulations, was cremated on the beach near Viareggio. http://en.wikipedia.org/wiki/Percy_Bysshe_Shelley**

BLUEBEARD
CHARLES PERRAULT

There was once a man who had fine houses, both in town and country, a deal of silver and gold plate, embroidered furniture, and coaches gilded all over with gold. But this man was so unlucky as to have a blue beard, which made him so frightfully ugly that all the women and girls ran away from him.

One of his neighbors, a lady of quality, had two daughters who were perfect beauties. He desired of her one of them in marriage, leaving to her choice which of the two she would bestow on him. Neither of them would have him, and they sent him backwards and forwards from one to the other, not being able to bear the thoughts of marrying a man who had a blue beard. Adding to their disgust and aversion was the fact that he already had been married to several wives, and nobody knew what had become of them.

Blue Beard, to engage their affection, took them, with their mother and three or four ladies of their acquaintance, with other young people of the neighborhood, to one of his country houses, where they stayed a whole week.

The time was filled with parties, hunting, fishing, dancing, mirth, and feasting. Nobody went to bed, but all passed the night in rallying and joking with each other. In short, everything succeeded so well that the youngest daughter began to think that the man's beard was not so very blue after all, and that he was a mighty civil gentleman.

As soon as they returned home, the marriage was concluded. About a month afterwards, Blue Beard told his wife that he was obliged to take a country journey for six weeks at least, about affairs of very great consequence. He desired her to divert herself in his absence, to send for her friends and acquaintances, to take them into the country, if she pleased, and to make good cheer wherever she was.

"Here," said he," are the keys to the two great wardrobes, wherein I have my best furniture. These are to my silver and gold plate, which is not everyday in use. These open my strongboxes, which hold my money, both gold and silver; these my caskets of jewels. And this is the master key to all my apartments. But as for this little one here, it is the key to the closet at the end of the great hall on the ground floor. Open them all; go into each and every one of them, except that little closet, which I forbid you, and forbid it in such a manner that, if you happen to open it, you may expect my just anger and resentment."

She promised to observe, very exactly, whatever he had ordered. Then he, after having embraced her, got into his coach and proceeded on his journey.

Her neighbors and good friends did not wait to be sent for by the newly married lady. They were impatient to see all the rich furniture of her house, and had not dared to come while her husband was there, because of his blue beard, which frightened them. They ran through all the rooms, closets, and wardrobes, which were all so fine and rich that they seemed to surpass one another.

After that, they went up into the two great rooms, which contained the best and richest furniture. They could not sufficiently admire the number and beauty of the tapestry, beds, couches, cabinets, stands, tables, and looking glasses, in which you might see yourself from head to foot; some of them were framed with glass, others with silver, plain and gilded, the finest and most magnificent that they had ever seen.

They ceased not to extol and envy the happiness of their friend, who in the meantime in no way diverted herself in looking upon all these rich things, because of the impatience she had to go and open the closet on the ground floor. She was so much pressed by her curiosity that, without considering that it was very uncivil for her to leave her company, she went down a little back staircase, and with such excessive haste that she nearly fell and broke her neck.

Having come to the closet door, she made a stop for some time, thinking about her husband's orders, and considering what unhappiness might attend her if she was disobedient; but the temptation was so strong that she could not overcome it. She then took the little key, and opened it, trembling. At first she could not see anything plainly, because the windows were shut. After some moments she began to perceive that the floor was all covered over with clotted blood, on which lay the bodies of several dead women, ranged against the walls. (These were all the wives whom Blue Beard had married and murdered, one after another.) She thought she should have died for fear, and the key, which she pulled out of the lock, fell out of her hand.

After having somewhat recovered her surprise, she picked up the key, locked the door, and went upstairs into her chamber to recover; but she could not, so much was she frightened. Having observed that the key to the closet was stained with blood, she tried two or three times to wipe it off; but the blood would not come out; in vain did she wash it, and even rub it with soap and sand. The blood still remained, for the key was magical and she could never make it quite clean; when the blood was gone off from one side, it came again on the other.

Blue Beard returned from his journey the same evening, saying that he had received letters upon the road, informing him that the affair he went about had concluded to his advantage. His wife did all she could to convince him that she was extremely happy about his speedy return.

The next morning he asked her for the keys, which she gave him, but with such a trembling hand that he easily guessed what had happened.

BLUEBEARD (continued)

"What!" said he, "is not the key of my closet among the rest?"

"I must," said she, "have left it upstairs upon the table."

"Fail not," said Blue Beard, "to bring it to me at once."

After several goings backwards and forwards, she was forced to bring him the key. Blue Beard, having very attentively considered it, said to his wife, "Why is there blood on the key?"

"I do not know," cried the poor woman, paler than death.

"You do not know!" replied Blue Beard. "I very well know. You went into the closet, did you not? Very well, madam; you shall go back, and take your place among the ladies you saw there."

Upon this she threw herself at her husband's feet, and begged his pardon with all the signs of a true repentance, vowing that she would never more be disobedient. She would have melted a rock, so beautiful and sorrowful was she; but Blue Beard had a heart harder than any rock!

"You must die, madam," said he, "at once."

"Since I must die," answered she (looking upon him with her eyes all bathed in tears), "give me some little time to say my prayers."

"I give you," replied Blue Beard, "half a quarter of an hour, but not one moment more."

When she was alone she called out to her sister, and said to her, "Sister Anne" (for that was her name), "go up, I beg you, to the top of the tower, and look if my brothers are not coming. They promised me that they would come today, and if you see them, give them a sign to make haste."

Her sister Anne went up to the top of the tower, and the poor afflicted wife cried out from time to time, "Anne, sister Anne, do you see anyone coming?"

And sister Anne said, "I see nothing but a cloud of dust in the sun, and the green grass."

In the meanwhile Blue Beard, holding a great sabre in his hand, cried out as loud as he could bawl to his wife, "Come down instantly, or I shall come up to you."

"One moment longer, if you please," said his wife; and then she cried out very softly, "Anne, sister Anne, do you see anybody coming?"

And sister Anne answered, "I see nothing but a cloud of dust in the sun, and the green grass."

"Come down quickly," cried Blue Beard, "or I will come up to you."

"I am coming," answered his wife; and then she cried, "Anne, sister Anne, do you not see anyone coming?"

"I see," replied sister Anne, "a great cloud of dust approaching us."

"Are they my brothers?"

"Alas, no my dear sister, I see a flock of sheep."

"Will you not come down?" cried Blue Beard.

"One moment longer," said his wife, and then she cried out, "Anne, sister Anne, do you see nobody coming?"

"I see," said she, "two horsemen, but they are still a great way off."

"God be praised," replied the poor wife joyfully. "They are my brothers. I will make them a sign, as well as I can for them to make haste."

Then Blue Beard bawled out so loud that he made the whole house tremble. The distressed wife came down, and threw herself at his feet, all in tears, with her hair about her shoulders.

"This means nothing," said Blue Beard. "You must die!" Then, taking hold of her hair with one hand, and lifting up the sword with the other, he prepared to strike off her head. The poor lady, turning about to him, and looking at him with dying eyes, desired him to afford her one little moment to recollect herself.

"No, no," said he, "commend yourself to God," and was just ready to strike.

At this very instant there was such a loud knocking at the gate that Blue Beard made a sudden stop. The gate was opened, and two horsemen entered. Drawing their swords, they ran directly to Blue Beard. He knew them to be his wife's brothers, one a dragoon, the other a musketeer; so that he ran away immediately to save himself; but the two brothers pursued and overtook him before he could get to the steps of the porch. Then they ran their swords through his body and left him dead. The poor wife was almost as dead as her husband, and had not strength enough to rise and welcome her brothers.

Blue Beard had no heirs, and so his wife became mistress of all his estate. She made use of one part of it to marry her sister Anne to a young gentleman who had loved her a long while; another part to buy captains' commissions for her brothers, and the rest to marry herself to a very worthy gentleman, who made her forget the ill time she had passed with Blue Beard.

ODE TO THE WEST WIND
PERCY BYSSHE SHELLEY

This poem was written in 1819 and published in 1820.

I.

WILD West Wind, thou breath of Autumn's being,
Thou, from whose unseen presence the leaves dead
Are driven, like ghosts from an enchanter fleeing,

Yellow, and black, and pale, and hectic red,
Pestilence-stricken multitudes: O thou,
Who chariotest to their dark wintry bed

The wingèd seeds, where they lie cold and low,
Each like a corpse within its grave, until
Thine azure sister of the spring shall blow

Her clarion o'er the dreaming earth, and fill
(Driving sweet buds like flocks to feed in air)
With living hues and odors plain and hill:

Wild Spirit, which art moving everywhere;
Destroyer and preserver; hear, oh, hear!

II.

Thou on whose stream, 'mid the steep
sky's commotion,
Loose clouds like earth's decaying leaves
are shed,
Shook from the tangled boughs of Heaven
and Ocean,

Angels of rain and lightning: there are spread
On the blue surface of thine airy surge,
Like the bright hair uplifted from the head

Of some fierce Mænad, even from the dim verge
Of the horizon to the zenith's height,
The locks of the approaching storm. Thou dirge

Of the dying year, to which this closing night
Will be the dome of a vast sepulchre,
Vaulted with all thy congregated might

Of vapors, from whose solid atmosphere
Black rain, and fire, and hail, will burst: oh hear!

III.

Thou who didst waken from his summer dreams
The blue Mediterranean, where he lay,
Lulled by the coil of his crystalline streams,

Beside a pumice isle in Baiæ's bay,
And saw in sleep old palaces and towers
Quivering within the wave's intenser day,

All overgrown with azure moss and flowers
So sweet, the sense faints picturing them! Thou
For whose path the Atlantic's level powers

Cleave themselves into chasms, while far below
The sea-blooms and the oozy woods which wear
The sapless foliage of the ocean, know

Thy voice, and suddenly grow gray with fear,
And tremble and despoil themselves:
oh, hear!

IV.

If I were a dead leaf thou mightest bear;
If I were a swift cloud to fly with thee;
A wave to pant beneath thy power, and share

The impulse of thy strength, only less free
Than thou, O uncontrollable! if even
I were as in my boyhood, and could be

The comrade of thy wanderings over heaven,
As then, when to outstrip thy skyey speed
Scarce seemed a vision; I would ne'er have striven

As thus with thee in prayer in my sore need.
Oh! lift me as a wave, a leaf, a cloud!
I fall upon the thorns of life! I bleed!

A heavy weight of hours has chained and bowed
One too like thee: tameless, and swift, and proud.

V.

Make me thy lyre, even as the forest is;
What if my leaves are falling like its own!
The tumult of thy mighty harmonies

Will take from both a deep, autumnal tone,
Sweet though in sadness. Be thou, Spirit fierce,
My spirit! Be thou me, impetuous one!

Drive my dead thoughts over the universe
Like withered leaves to quicken a new birth!
And, by the incantation of this verse,

Scatter, as from an extinguished hearth
Ashes and sparks, my words among mankind!
Be through my lips to unwakened earth

The trumpet of a prophecy! O Wind,
If Winter comes, can Spring be far behind?

COMIC PAGE GRID

COMIC SCRIPT - VOLUME II CHAPTER VIII

Panel 1
In the foreground, the man has the girl now in his arms. She has slightly revived, her own arms wrapped around his neck. This should suggest that he is her father. He is running with her away from the MONSTER, who is pursuing them into the wood.

	ORIGINAL TEXT	QUICK TEXT
CAPTION MONSTER V/O	Tearing the girl from my arms, he hastened towards the deeper parts of the wood. I followed speedily, I hardly knew why.	Tearing the girl from my arms, he ran back into the woods; and I followed them.

Panel 2
There is still a distance of some yards between them. The man has put his daughter gently on the ground. She is dazed, but sitting, coming around. He has his rifle in his hands and is aiming it at the MONSTER, who is still running towards him.

CAPTION MONSTER V/O	When he saw me draw near, he aimed a gun...	When he saw me drawing near, he aimed his gun at me...

Panel 3
The man fires, the bullet (a metal ball in those days) entering and passing through the MONSTER's right shoulder. This knocks him backwards through the air and he cries out in pain.

CAPTION MONSTER V/O	...and fired!	...and fired!
SFX (from the gun)	KRAKK!	KRAKK!
MONSTER	ARRGH!	ARRGH!
CAPTION MONSTER V/O	I sank to the ground and my injurer escaped into the wood.	I sank to the ground and the man escaped into the wood.

Panel 4
Close up of the MONSTER lying on the ground, his left hand clawing at the air around the wound on his right shoulder. His face is a grimace of agony.

CAPTION MONSTER V/O	I had saved a human being from destruction, and as a recompense I now writhed under the miserable pain of a wound which shattered the flesh and bone! The feelings of kindness gave place to hellish rage. Inflamed by pain, I vowed eternal hatred and vengeance to all mankind!	I'd saved someone's life and as a reward, I had a shattering wound. In great pain, I vowed eternal hatred and vengeance to all mankind.

EDUCATIONAL WEBSITE LINKS

PROMOTING LITERACY IN THE CLASSROOM:-

The Graphic Classroom
http://graphicclassroom.blogspot.com/

The Graphic Classroom is a resource for teachers and librarians to help them stock high quality, educational-worthy, graphic novels and comics in their classroom or school library.

Expanding Literacies through Graphic Novels
www.readwritethink.org/lessons/lesson_view.asp?id=1102

Gretchen Schwarz offers a rationale, based on the need for current students to learn multiple literacies, for the use of graphic novels in the high school English class. She highlights several titles, suggests possible classroom strategies, and discusses some of the obstacles teachers may face in adding graphic novels to their curriculum. **Gretchen E. Schwarz**

Eek! Comics in the Classroom!
www.education-world.com/a_curr/profdev/profdev105.shtml

More and more teachers are finding that once-maligned comics, and their big brothers graphic novels, can be effective tools for teaching a multitude of literacy skills to students with a variety of learning needs. **Education World**

Comics in Education
www.humblecomics.com/comicsedu/

The potency of the picture story is not a matter of modern theory but of anciently established truth. Before man thought in words, he felt in pictures. **Gene Yang**

Going Graphic - Comics at Work in the Multilingual Classroom
http://college.heinemann.com/shared/onlineresources/E00475/chapter2.pdf

Theory, research, practice, guidelines and resources for using comics and graphic novels in the classroom. **Stephen Cary**

Graphic Novels - a visual literary art form
www.clermont.lib.oh.us/teensite/teengraphicnov.html

What is most exciting is that a picture language and a word language can interweave, which can't be done by either one alone." **Will Eisner, Clermont County Public Library**

The Secret Origin of Good Readers
www.night-flight.com/secretorigin/index.html

Discusses how teachers, librarians, retailers, and publishers can work together to bring comic books into the classroom for use as an innovative and motivating cross-curricular teaching tool and a vehicle for promoting reading and literacy.

EDUCATIONAL WEBSITE LINKS

GENERAL GRAPHIC NOVEL SITES:-

Graphic Novel Review Site for Teens
www.noflyingnotights.com
Covers everything from superheroes to historical novels via Manga and cartoons. **Robin Brenner**

Comics Worth Reading
http://comicsworthreading.com
Independent Opinions by Johanna Draper Carlson and friends
News and reviews of graphic novels, manga, comic books, and related subjects